Walking in Both Worlds

Personal Stories and Practical Guidance on Spiritual Development

Natha Jay

Library of Congress Control Number: 2018914368

ISBN-13: 978-0-578-42459-0

Imprint: 1824988

Cover and text design by Janet Bergin,
empoweryourawesomeness.com

Dyslexia friendly font thanks to DylexieFont.com

To JC
For building the launching pad with me.

TABLE OF CONTENTS

Self-Care
Being Fully Human
Integration of the Trinity
Deep Healing

CHAPTER 5. EXPRESSION 67

~LOVE SPELLS~

Talk & Listen
Speaking Your Truth
Trust, Betrayal, and Forgiveness
Creation & Creativity
New Vocabulary

CHAPTER 6. INTENTION 85

~ACCIDENTAL UPGRADE~

Memory
Loyalty & Accountability
Judgment & Discernment
Epiphany
The Eternal Now

CHAPTER 7. CONNECTION 101

~A DAY IN THE LIFE~

In Service to Love
Active Surrender
Absolute Accountability
Alignment
Breath of God

INTRODUCTION

It's funny that the first phrases that come to my mind, when I think of Natha and her writing, are "practical" and "down to earth". It's funny because Natha writes and teaches on topics of extreme esoterica, interdimensional consciousness, and deep teachings of the mystery schools, that are far from conventional. Yet, she discusses and explains these things with the plain-spoken straight forwardness of someone who simply lives and breathes in both worlds.

Natha calls her blog "Walking in Both Worlds". That title suggests there are two worlds, and for most people there may seem a separation between "the seen and unseen". For Natha, though, I think it's just one world that includes all of it. For her, none of it is entirely "unseen". That's why she can talk about these things with simplicity and clarity.

So many people are starting to wake up right now. Maybe it's a tipping point of collective consciousness, collective ascension, divine or other-worldly intervention, or inevitable evolution. Maybe all of that. I don't know for sure. Even though I'm not sure of how or why, I can see it happening and it's both thrilling and disorienting.

That's why we're lucky when someone like Natha comes out a bit ahead of the pack, to offer clear headed guidance from her own experience. It helps to know you're not alone, and even if you are on a road less traveled, you don't have to clear the path all by yourself.

Tracy Roe, author
The Mature Empath

Foreword

You are not alone.

This mass awakening is shaking the very foundations of what we previously considered reality. From personal beliefs to societal structures to the very planet, it's all shifting. Destruction? Rebirth? Yes. You can't have one without the other.

I focused on the beginning questions of awakening in my first book, *Waking Up Indigo*. Now we go a little deeper into the personal, spiritual journey. This book assumes the reader has done enough ego (shadow) work to grasp more subtle wisdom. That said, if these topics seem to be irrelevant at the moment, try the other book. I want everyone to have access to helpful information, wherever they are on the journey.

There are many pitfalls along the path of awakening, and I have tried to point out the ones I've found, in the hope you can avoid the sticky spots. Knowledge is power, and this knowledge is meant to empower your journey.

Practical note: I recommend you read this book as you see fit. Cover-to-cover, random pages, a break between each chapter, whatever. There is a lot of subtle information here, so absorb it, as you need to. It is interspersed with personal stories, for your entertainment. Yes, they are all true.

This book is for all of us awakening at this time. And awakening isn't a singular event; it is a constant unfolding of higher truths. If you are drawn to this book, the Universe is beckoning you to remember who you really are, with the assurance that you are not alone.

And together we change the world.

PHYSICALITY

CHAPTER 1 – PHYSICALITY

~ Predators & Prey ~

At one point, I had a real job at a corporate office. One fine day when I stepped in the front door, a man with an Irish accent greeted me. Because of a neurological disability I look down at my feet when I walk, to be sure I know where they are. When he said hello, I looked up and made eye contact. My first thought was Yikes! *Sure am glad I'm not sweet and innocent!*

Upon making that assessment, I made sure to keep eye contact, walked right up to him, stood a little too close, and joined him in small talk about the weather and work and such. After less than a minute he decided I wasn't what he was looking for, and wandered back to his cubicle. Of course, I let him end the conversation, and step away first.

Crisis averted! I kind of felt like I needed a shower at that point, but the mission was accomplished... these are not the droids you're looking for... or at least, this one will be more trouble than she's worth. I never saw him (Gus from HR) again. But he soon made quite the stir...

A couple months later, I go into my department, and the office gossip ran up to me before I could even get my coat off...

"You know Gus from HR?"

"Who?"

"Gus! The guy with the Irish accent!"

"Oh, right, Gus. Yeah, I know Gus."

"Well, he didn't show up for work yesterday. No call or anything. And today the FBI was here! They want to extradite him to stand trial for 19 counts of pedophilia!"

"Okay. And?"

"And??? Who would've guessed? It's Gus! He's the nicest guy! I never would have suspected!"

And this is where I got really curious. I knew from the moment we made eye contact that he was a predator. I even knew he was looking for sweet, innocent victims. Did people just love the drama, or did they truly not know? Were some people more prone to being victimized? I pondered this one for months, watching people interact, watching their body language, watching their energy. I read somewhere that animals hunting in the wild analyze energy, not the factors we use (age, illness, speed). This makes way more sense to me.

I suspect that the world consists of two major groups: predators and prey. Predators are constantly evaluating the energies around them, while prey have no idea this is happening. If you had no idea this was happening, don't worry too much. From my limited observations, some people who are definitely in the 'prey' category use body language to compensate. They can be less vulnerable due to good posture, strong eye contact, and general openness. And if you are on the predator end of things, it doesn't automatically mean you will use your skills to harm others. In this context, I am simply saying that some people perceive things on a different level.

I also suspect that most predators and prey are acting on a subconscious level. Gus had no idea that I could see his intentions at first glance, nor what I was doing to dissuade him. Awareness is everything. But even though my actions were conscious, it was instinct that told me what to do. So what does that make me?

Not prey.

A WORD ABOUT WORDS

Words are just symbols we use to communicate an experience, nothing more. Without telepathy, we are left to verbally describe our experience, within the bounds of language. Because of this, word definition is vital to accurate communication. A good amount of argument is simply misunderstanding.

Several years ago, I was having a wonderful time speaking to a new coworker about our views on life. We had so much in common, he asked me what church I attended. I then used a word, which to me meant "tree-hugging, dirt-worshiping hippie", but to him meant "devil worshiper". Now that's an awkward, and abrupt, end to an otherwise lovely conversation. He refused to speak to me for days. On my day off, another coworker explained what I had meant, but it was still a fragile relationship for several weeks. The word in question was, "Pagan".

To complicate matters, even the dictionary definitions of words change over time. Take this sentence: "I am content with my small house." What does that mean to you? "Content" was once defined as "perfectly happy", but has now become "it'll do". I know this because I have a friend that I've never communicated well with, to the point of needing a dictionary on a regular basis. Sometimes two. I just happen to have my Grandparent's old one. There have been lots of changes to word use, and definition, over the years.

Now consider the word, "Christian". This word covers beliefs ranging from Unitarian to Catholic to Jehovah's Witnesses, and hundreds more. When someone tells me they are Christian, all I know for sure is that the main god is Yahweh, and Jesus in involved at some level. It doesn't even mean they believe in heaven, hell, or having a soul... all the things most people assume of Christians. Similarly, an "Atheist" simply doesn't believe in an external, personified deity, but may be deeply spiritual. We do our best with the words we have, but a single word rarely adequately describes an experience.

Add to that the changing of word definition to cater to the ego of the user. This one is a pet peeve of mine in the spiritual arena. "Tantra" has always been an ancient and sacred energy practice, but now is used in all kinds of sexuality classes, including how to have better orgasms. "Polyamory" means "many loves", but now is applied to promiscuity by meaning "many sex partners". "New Age" used to refer to the evolution of humanity, but now it's equated to denial (it's all God, so it's all good). You get the point. Without telepathy, we really need to define our words to have any meaningful exchange.

Plus, as human experience expands, we simply need new words to describe it. Ask fifteen people to define "love", and you'll get fifteen answers. We use the word "pedophile" to describe both people who rape toddlers, and those who seduce 17-year-olds. Those are definitely significantly different situations, yet our vocabulary tries to put them under the same word. Humanity's highest achievements, and its lowest depravities, need more words to accurately describe the experiences being had.

So, the two things worth noting here are honesty and curiosity.

Be honest, with yourself and others, by saying what you really mean, not using the fashionable euphemism. Just own it, whatever it is, and be willing to speak openly about it. If you are hesitant to use words that actually describe the experience, rather than some softer version of half-truth, then that tells you that you just aren't comfortable being honest with yourself. What are you hiding? What are you justifying? How are you deceiving yourself? It's better to face those shadows, than to spread them with half-truths.

Be curious, with your own definitions and with others', rather than assuming what is meant. Labels are shorthand, not the finished document. Be open to learning, to asking questions. People are always more complex and interesting than the labels that they identify with. Your own beliefs are worth examining, defining, and then redefining, as you grow. Before you react, ask, "What does that word mean to you?" The answer might surprise you.

And by the way, Pagans don't believe in the devil.

"I like the word 'indolence'.
It makes my laziness seem classy."
~ Bernard Williams

"One of the definitions of sanity is
the ability to tell real from unreal.
Soon we'll need a new definition."
~ Alvin Toffler

WHAT IF?

There is so much potential in us, and the only limits are our beliefs. I invite you to play a little game with me called "What If?" It should be played for at least a few days to be effective. It's simple... every time you have a solid idea about your world, form that opinion into a question, and then also ask the opposite question. For example, let's say I think my religion is the best one... I ask these two questions: "What if my religion is the only right one?" and also "What if it's not?" Don't justify an answer either way, just ask the question, and then let it go.

Certainty is the mortal enemy of possibility. This game is about questions, not answers. In fact, if you find yourself justifying a belief, the game ends, and you must start over. Look at everything with the fresh eyes of wonder. Ready? Let's play!

What if I'm on my spiritual path? What if I'm not? What if all gods and goddesses are mythological and symbolic? What if they aren't? What if there's an afterlife? What if there isn't? What if psychic ability is related to insanity? What if it isn't? What if every person in my life has played their part perfectly? What if they didn't?

What if the climate is changing? What if it isn't? What if western medicine is helping prevent illness? What if it's not? What if the USA is the best place to live? What if it's not? What if voting really changes laws? What if it doesn't? What if money is the backbone of civilization? What if it isn't? What if conspiracy theories are real? What if they aren't?

What if we are living in a virtual reality game? What if we aren't? What if we can get to the level of programmer? What if we can't? What if the masses suddenly awaken? What if they don't? What if this is all there is to life? What if it isn't? What if hedonism is entirely selfish? What if it isn't?

What if morality is just social conditioning? What if it isn't?

What if I have more to offer the world? What if I don't? What if I am living to the fullest? What if I'm not? What if I could heal myself on all levels? What if I can't? What do I want to be when I grow up? What if that ship has sailed?

Allow the possibility of possibility to flow through you. Maybe look a little deeper at areas you get stuck on. Once you are certain about anything, it becomes your prison, stunting future growth. In quantum physics, that's when the wave turns into a particle - a solid thing to bump against. When you allow yourself to be a bit unsure, you allow the Mystery of life to flow. What if you were open to the Universe surprising you? What if...?

"Stop thinking in terms of limitations and start thinking in terms of possibilities."
~ Terry Josephson

"Recently, I have taken as my personal mantra the not very transcendent phrase, 'I don't know.' The list of things that I feel unsure about seems to be steadily increasing."
~ Daniel Pinchbeck

SPIRITUAL FOUNDATION

There has been much distress caused by **New Age** spirituality only focusing on love and light, while ignoring the shadow side. While this is true, I wish to offer another perspective. What if, instead of blatant denial, we needed this unbalanced approach to wake people up? For some, it is the concept of love and light and bliss and oneness that make them start to consider something bigger than their conditioning. It served a purpose.

I know a teacher that says her calling is to take humans and teach them to be gods - to wake people up. Hard job, but totally necessary. My calling is to take gods and teach them how to be human. I work with people who are already awake, and struggling with integration of light and dark, of soul and ego. This is why so much of my writing has to do with the ego, and shadow work. Okay, my beautiful gods and goddesses, let's look at the foundation of being a spiritual human...
The **New Age** stuff starts at the top (oneness, unconditional love), and works down, like a trickle-down spirituality. Works about as well in the long run as trickle-down economics, but at least it wakes people up. The only way to actually attain those spiritual goals (yes, it's totally possible) is to build from the ground up, starting with a firm foundation. *Boundaries and discernment are essential to personal and spiritual growth.* Without boundaries you are open to abuse of all kinds. Without discernment you are open to addiction of all kinds.

Boundaries are about self-knowledge, and what you are willing to allow in your life. So many people are stressed out because they keep attracting the same kind of partner or job. I am less interested in what they attract, and more interested in how they handle it. Do they see the pattern? Do they walk away from abusive situations? Only you can say "no" to a situation. By doing nothing but complaining about it, you are telling the Universe, "Yes, please, more of this!" Working from the top down, you visualize what you DO want. Working from a foundation of firm boundaries, you walk away from what you DON'T want. Keep saying, "no", until you can say, "this, or better".

Discernment is about staying on your path. No one is passing judgment on you, yet there are things that will evolve you and things that won't, and everyone is different. Working from the top down, everything is of the Light, therefore, everything is good. Working from a foundation of discernment, things are equal but different, and you have the responsibility of choice (free will). You can choose to live on fast food and never exercise, or you can choose to eat raw food and do yoga everyday. They are both valid choices, but will result in very different life experiences. Free will matters. Discernment matters. Whatever will evolve you, choose that.
A couple of traps to avoid...

Hedonism isn't a spiritual path. Enjoying physical pleasure is fine, but when it becomes the goal of existence, you are off path. Human bodies are prone to addiction, and pleasure-seeking encourages that.

Learning from a teacher is different than following a guru. If there is pressure to stay with a teacher, or if you feel like you couldn't live without them, then check your boundaries.

Learning a lesson isn't the same as tolerating abuse. The biggest lesson of an abusive relationship is learning how to walk away. Building strong boundaries is necessary. No one can grow until they feel safe.

Struggling with life issues isn't a sign of failure. We are meant to "wrestle with God", or have growing pains. God comforts the disturbed, and disturbs the comfortable... Growing pains indicate growth, rather than decay.

Yes, there are many other layers to your personal development, but the foundation is always important. Only you can say, "no" to situations that are hurting you or limiting your

9

growth. Only you can discern what choices will keep you on your path. Life is waiting for you to take these steps, and build your own foundation to your Inner Temple.

"We need discernment in what we see and what we hear and what we believe."
~ Charles R. Swindoll

"We are not human beings having a spiritual experience. We are spiritual beings having a human experience."
~ Pierre Teilhard de Chardin

REVISITING MORALITY

I don't believe in Divine Judgment, but I am a firm believer that humans misinterpret things on a regular basis. No higher authority is judging your actions, but it is just as incorrect to say, "it's all God, so it's all good", and then make poor choices. Free will most definitely matters, and some choices will evolve you, while others won't. What if moral teachings in religion were really just tips on how to evolve more efficiently? What if the Mystery School teachings are hidden by dogma? Let's take another look at morality.

Remove all judgments, of yourself and others, and look at these concepts with fresh eyes. Keep your mind open, and just ponder the possibilities...

I have always joked that my life is a delicate balance of the seven deadly sins... sloth and gluttony are always in the lead, but thankfully vanity takes a close third. The seven deadly sins are a Catholic adaptation of older lists of vices, and the current interpretation of the list varies a bit, but I will discuss the list as I remember it. Remember, this isn't about which "sins" are named, it's about seeing morality in a different light.

Sloth - What if this is about being lazy, not with outward action, but with doing inner work? What if it warns about being stagnant in our personal growth?

Gluttony - What if this warns about the danger of addiction? Too much of a good thing is never a good thing. Hedonism (living solely for the pursuit of physical pleasure) falls under this title.

Vanity - What if this is about being ego-bound, and totally self-involved? Our current definition of "toxic person" or "narcissist" falls in this category.

Pride - What if this is simply about separation? If I think I'm better than you, I am setting myself up to be alone.

Wrath (Vengeance) - What if this is about judgment and

projection? Throwing our baggage on other people, instead of owning our reactions. Or, maybe to warn against victim mentality, and using blame instead of making boundaries.

Greed - What if this warns about living from a sense of lack? Or, maybe to remind us that we can all live by sharing, but only a few benefit from hoarding.

Envy (Jealously) - What if this warns of the pitfall of looking outside oneself for validation? Constantly searching for happiness and wholeness on the outside, and through comparison.

Most Mystery School teachings are hidden in a backward form like this. Instead of "don't be prideful", read it as "remember you are One". So, what would the opposites be? What are the seven life-affirming messages? Here's one possibility...

Sloth becomes Seeker (do your inner work)

Gluttony becomes Discernment (make choices that evolve you)

Vanity becomes Inspired (being your true and unique self, which can't be compared)

Pride becomes Oneness (we are all on separate, but equal, paths to the same Source)

Wrath becomes Forgiveness (of self and others, and reclaiming personal power)

Greed becomes Generosity (everyone wins when we share)

Envy becomes Introspection (look within, not outside yourself)

When you consider these "sins" from a more mystical angle, what lessons do you see? What pitfalls are they warning against? In what way are they trying to give you guidance to make life easier, to promote evolution?

And what about marriage and monogamy? What if "marriage" represents commitment, and "monogamy" is about discernment? What if sexual energy is so powerful it should be handled carefully, and treated as sacred? What if these concepts have nothing to do with right and wrong, but only proper use of energy?

And the three Graces - Charm, Beauty, and Creativity? All three are developed from within. Charm could be the magnetic field of an open heart. Beauty might be the spark of an awakened eye. Creativity is the divinity of humanity... that's why kids love art projects.

Much to ponder here. All I know for sure is that literal interpretations of Divine writings are always brutal. Let the Mystery of life come through everything, and revisit your beliefs often.

"Aim above morality. Be not simply good, be good for something."
~ Henry David Thoreau

"Just assume the answer to every question is compassion."
~ Author Unknown

SUBCONSCIOUS

CHAPTER 2 - SUBCONSCIOUS

~ Ghosts & Dead Babies ~

I have the best adventures with Tyler! We are really only distant friends, but whenever we come together, there's a great story to tell. Like these two...

I first met Tyler through a mutual friend, who invited me to my first mala making class, at Tyler's house, which also happened to have a ghost problem. She wanted us to meet in a casual setting, while letting me get a feel for the ghost, to see if I could help. All through the class, I felt a small child peering curiously around the corner, but he would hide every time I focused my attention on him.

After the class, when everyone else had gone, I talked to Tyler about the young ghost. As we talked, I kept hearing the song Oh Danny Boy in my head, so I asked, "Was he Irish, or was his name Danny? I keep hearing Oh Danny Boy." She turned pale white, and said, "His name was Daniel." Apparently, she had already had a psychic give her enough detail to do some research. He was a 4-year-old, drowned in the tub by his mother about a hundred years ago, thus all the issues she was having with the plumbing. Well, at least we were talking about the same ghost.

Now, how to get him to move on? Tyler had already tried several times with several people, including a priest. I set up an ascension pillar, but Danny wouldn't go near it. He was terrified, poor thing. He didn't trust it or me. I suppose being drowned by one's own mother would leave a mark. Trust issues are justified at that point. I decided to go home, meditate on it, and work remotely.

In meditation, I was told to try a psych-k balance, used to clear trauma from the subconscious. It works great on the living, but I'd never tried it on the dead. Worth a shot. After I did my normal protocols to get hooked up to him, I did a few balances for trust. I was just thinking to myself, how will I know when he's ready? Suddenly, walked right into the ascension tube, and up he went. Well, there it is. He was greeted by his friends in a celebration of his return. None of them said thanks, or even acknowledged my part in it at all. Was it just a given that I should help? Did they know that help was given? Could they even see me? It really gave me a lot to think about.

The effects were immediate. Tyler's kids and dog were no longer on edge, and the plumbing calmed right down and behaved normally. I've only run across a couple true ghosts, and really, they just want to go home.

•••

A few years later, Tyler contacted me again. This time, she was ready to sell her ghost-free house, but it wouldn't budge. The market was on fire, and homes were being sold hours after listing... but not her house. It was a beautiful home, in a great area, for a reasonable price, yet it had been shown 48 times without any offers.

Tyler explained it all to me, and asked if I could just take a peek remotely to see if there was still an entity issue or something. I agreed, and when I meditated that afternoon I looked in energetically. I got the image of a dead baby buried in the yard. Well, you can't say that out loud, can you? I just told her the house seemed fine, but maybe the yard... was there anything buried in the yard?

"My baby! My baby!" she replied. Whew! At least I didn't have to say it! She said her beloved cat was buried there. And after thinking about it, she remembered planting her placenta from her son's birth with the tree out front. And now we have two dead babies, of sorts. On the right track! It seemed like the house couldn't sell because she had (completely unconscious) energetic attachments to that yard. I told her to do a ritual, releasing all things in the yard to Gaia... let Mother Earth reclaim it all. I just gave her the outline and intention, and she devised the actual ritual.

Within a week an offer was made, and the house was sold. Attachment, even unconscious, really matters. And conscious intention can move mountains... and sell houses.

"Our feet are planted in the real world, but we dance with angels and ghosts."
~ John Cameron Mitchell

KARMA (PART I)

Most people consider karma to be a system of punishment and reward, basically just like heaven and hell, but during our Earthly existence. But that would require judgment of right & wrong, and then we need someone to do the judging. It gets weird really quickly. The Universe is beautiful in its simplicity, and so is karma.

Karma is just a vibration. Vibration can be changed with awareness and choice. Living within a given vibration allows you to group with other people and circumstances of that same vibration. If you smoke, you will attract others who smoke, or at least treat their body the same way. If you meditate, you will attract others who connect to the inner self. It may not always look the same on the outside (one of my very best friends is quite Christian, and I am anything but), but you will both be working at the same level (in this case, love). So, if you are surrounded by addicts, some part of you believes deeply in disempowerment, even if you have no addictions of your own.

To clean up your karma simply means to raise your vibration in order to leave that pattern behind. In this time of ascension, the vibration of the collective is being raised. Thus, many of us are seeing our karmic patterns up close and personal, whether we want to or not. To those who are really attached to their stories, it feels like the world is ending, because those attachments have to go. To those who have dedicated themselves to understanding their attachments, it feels like heaven, because those attachments have to go. Awareness is everything. Be really observant of yourself and where you aren't comfortable, and be willing to release those attachments. This might mean forgiving, or having better boundaries, or loving yourself unconditionally. We're all different, and need different things. Know thyself.

A word of warning - you can only change your own karma.

You must be willing to release anyone at anytime. Basically, just love people, but don't get attached to a story about your relationship. You can't make others evolve. We are all moving at our own pace, and "holding space" for them is exhausting for the higher vibe, and annoying for the lower vibe. Just do your thing, and allow people to come and go from your life. This is normal, and it may seem like a revolving door, if you are rising quickly. Your body will tell you if you are surround- ed by higher or lower vibrations - listen to it. If you are the brightest light in the room, it's time to find a different room.

Attachments are highlighted by emotional reactions. Look at where you have the most dramatic emotional responses to find your greatest attachments. Attachment just means belief in an ego story. If you have a strong belief in "someday my prince/princess will come", then you will have a strong emo- tional response whenever that story is threatened. Anything less than unconditional love will bring some kind of emotional reaction. Look for your stronger reactions, and that's where to start unwinding the attachments.

When I was a teenager, my Grandma used to warn me about falling in with the wrong crowd. I always replied, "Jesus hung out with lepers and prostitutes, and he turned out ok." I have always disliked the idea of judgment, but several de- cades later, I see it in a whole new light. Some of the kindest, most openhearted people I know are the outcasts of society. Maybe Jesus was hanging out with really high vibe folks who just didn't fit in. I recommend you find high vibe (low karma) people, to make the ascension process easier.

No one is judging you, and there is no battle of good and evil. In fact, try changing two words in your vocabulary: Change "karma" to "vibration", and change "evil" to "ego". "I must have good money *vibration*." "Lord, deliver me from ego." It's so much more accurate. Stay aware. Watch your attachments. Let people, situations, and things come and go. Now is the time to release the old, and build the new karma... I mean, vibration.

KARMA (PART II)

Ever have one of those days when the voices in your head just won't stop talking? *sigh* Apparently, I missed a few things about karma.

We live in the time-space continuum, which is the 3rd & 4th dimensions, but Gaia (with all her inhabitants) is ascending to the 5th dimension. The time-space continuum is basically our veil, allowing us to experience an existence separate from the whole. Our ego allows this separation on an individual level. Both individual and collective veils are dissolving to allow for the ascension process to continue, which is a perfectly normal evolutionary change. It just seems "out there" because the ego has done such a great job keeping us in the dark, so to speak.

As these veils soften, we naturally return to a collective. First we have increased awareness, then increased compassion, then opening of psychic abilities, telepathy, and eventually union with our Higher Selves. What's left? Not much that muggles (non-magic folk) value. All the stories leave. No more drive for power. It's all replaced with what we call Unconditional Love. Love is literally the only thing going with you. Forgive everything else to ease the process. This doesn't mean we won't have to work to reach a place of forgiveness, just that it's worth it.

Karma (vibrational attachments) are tied to time, the 4th dimension. If you think about any trigger you have, it is either a reminder of the past or a fear of the future. You can definitely have emotional disturbances that are limited to the present moment, but they also pass quickly, just like the present moment. The 5th dimension is beyond distance and time as we now experience it. It's more of an eternal "here & now". The attachment to stories and expectations that take us out of the now, are leaving. It's getting really hard to hold a grudge.

Also remember that your stories are giving you practice at

being in a certain vibration. You will naturally want to return there, until you become aware (conscious) of what's happening. For example, "someday my prince will come" is practicing waiting and longing. So, when the prince shows up, you have no practice being happy. That story is also based in the future, which never comes, because we only live **NOW.** Your stories aren't who you are, just who you've practiced being. It's ok to change them.

The ego, therefore karma, is very tied to the body and the physical experience. Those who have become slaves to the body, seeking pleasure for pleasure's sake, will notice a radical shift. In order for these karmic layers to dissolve, we will start to recognize the body as a temple, not a playground. Same with the body of Gaia. We are suddenly realizing, as a collective, how sacred She is, and our part in honoring Her. This same shift is also altering our attachment to sex, especially when used primarily as physical pleasure. Deep conversations are becoming more valuable than sex. Let your sex drive change. Your whole body is changing.

Upgrades to basic body chemistry are happening rapidly. There's a reason for sometimes craving fruit juice and dark chocolate. It really makes me wonder what part of this would show up on a blood test... not enough to go in and ask, but I do wonder. Sleep is also greatly affected. Sometimes 4 hours is plenty, sometimes 10 isn't enough. Be where you are, and honor your process.

And most of all, we are still human. Releasing karma is messy. Ego work takes dedication. This stuff is for the warriors of awareness. It all comes down to forgiveness. After you manage to forgive others, then the tough part comes up. You must forgive yourself. Forgive yourself for having bad boundaries, for not communicating, for staying too long, for leaving too soon, for setting expectations others could never meet. Forgive yourself for not knowing any better. It's a lot. Just know the energy is so supportive of this work. And you have an invisible team with you at all times. You are so very loved, and truly you are Love. Welcome home.

"Karma is experience, and experience creates
memory, and memory creates imagination and
desire, and desire creates karma again.
If I buy a cup of coffee, that's karma.
I now have that memory that might give me
the potential desire for having cappuccino,
and I walk into Starbucks, and
there's karma all over again."
~ Deepak Chopra

SUPPRESSION & EXCESS

Humans are higher consciousness beings living in an animal body. We have collectively made certain decisions, in certain societal constructs, that our animal nature is vulgar, and best to be avoided. If it was taught to us in a more direct way, it really wouldn't be a problem, but it isn't. We have lost the art of symbology, so are left with a gross misrepresentation of the actual point.

Usually, when we are confronted by our animal nature, we look at our tribal knowledge, and suppress any "inappropriate" urges. This is perhaps most easily exemplified by our sexual desires and religion. We have lost the original directive of using some discernment regarding our sexual behavior (which most animals lack), and replaced it with a dogma of shame, guilt, and fear. Truly unfortunate, and not what was intended.

Suppression is the burial of a conscious thought or feeling that we choose to bury in hopes that it will simply disappear. This never works. It either comes leaking out around the edges under cover of secrecy, or it simply explodes into excess of the very urge being suppressed. The third option is that it is stored in the body, causing all kinds of health issues. It really is so much easier to face it head-on, and I wish religion allowed for this to happen without fear of punishment.

Staying with the example of sex, the secrecy side leads to pedophile priests, a huge porn industry, and prostitution. The explosion of excess is seen in the growing number of groups trying to normalize, or even spiritualize, sexual pleasure without commitment. Before we go on, I am not personally against religion, polyamory, or alternative sexuality; I just feel that both sides of the coin have missed the actual point. There truly is a point, and it lies in the potential of being fully human, not just an animal with control issues.

The view of most religions is to control behavior with fear - a loving god, who will torture you for all eternity if you even think the wrong thing. Of course you are going to think the wrong thing. Your body is an animal that just wants to ensure there are children to continue the species. I know people who absolutely can't stand silence, for fear their thoughts will cost them an eternity in hell. There always has to be background noise to distract them. I can think of nothing further from god than being unable to be at peace in your own mind.

People eventually get tired of being emotionally controlled by fear and shame, so they go to the other extreme. They want to experience the pleasure of the senses in any way they can, without regard for themselves or others. It's usually a self-destructive path, while also being quite selfish. This is the root of hedonism, which is seeking physical pleasure in any form (food, sex, drugs, etc.) as the end goal of life. These folks have never been taught moderation or discernment, only suppression and judgment. It can take a bit for the pendulum to return to center.

And people usually find center in the end. Swinging to extremes isn't normally the issue; it's getting lost at either end that creates the problems. Being terrified of divine consequences (based on human misinterpretation) will eventually take a toll on the health of the body because of suppression. The swing into excess can lead to denial and addiction, also taking a toll on the health. Pleasure (fleeting experience) is easily confused with joy (a state of being).

So, where do we start to change this cycle? Start wherever you are, of course. On a grand scale, I would love to see religion embrace symbolism again. Just like Santa Claus symbolically represents the spirit of giving, god/goddess represents our own divine spark. There isn't literally a fat guy in a red suit breaking into your house and leaving presents, and there isn't literally an old man sitting on a cloud passing judgment on your every thought. Just as these personifications are only symbolic, so are the religious directives for our lives. Reread your religious text of choice, and actively search for the symbolism. Maybe marriage just means commitment. Maybe hell is just denial of your own divinity. Maybe all the "rules" started off as reminders we can be more than animals.

For those on the swing of excess, keep in mind there is a middle ground. Leave the concept of sin and judgment, but know that living for physical pleasure alone won't fulfill you. Humans are both animal and spiritual, and need both to feel complete. You can explore within safe boundaries, when you are ready to set them for yourself. You can receive honest guidance, when you are willing to listen. Discernment isn't the same as judgment. Allow yourself to swing back to center.

To reach our human potential, we need to fully recognize the two energies swirling within us. We are each the spark of god wrapped in a cute, little animal body. We have animal urges, but also access to a Higher Mind to allow for discernment, and free will actions. Neither one is bad, but our potential lies in the integration of the two. Can you make choices without judging yourself? Do you rely on dogma instead of your internal compass to tell right from wrong? Are you supporting the health of the body, or are you addicted to physical stimulation?

The nice thing is that both parts are fully supporting you. Your body is always striving for health, and your spirit is always striving to be in body. It's only the ego, with its stories, getting in the way. Only you know where you are, only you can change your course, and only you can integrate your being. Awareness is everything. Be honest with yourself on this one. You know the way, just keep going.

"Use, do not abuse... neither abstinence
nor excess ever renders man happy."
~ Voltaire

VICTIM MENTALITY

We tend to think of victim mentality with a flare of the dramatic... "Oh, poor me!" But it's considerably more subtle and elusive. Anytime we feel powerless, we are feeling the effects of being a victim of circumstance. While we can't change some circumstances, we can always adjust our mentality. Well, almost always. Let's take a brief look at mental illness...

While mental illness has many complexities, which I am not qualified to discuss, there are two main categories to be aware of for our purposes: cognitive and physical. With a cognitive disorder, wrong thinking creates physical change (anxiety caused by thoughts can increased heart rate), and the person can benefit greatly from cognitive therapy, where they can learn coping skills. With a physical disorder, physical changes cause wrong thinking (like Alzheimer's or schizophrenia), where cognitive therapy is of little use, because the physical brain no longer functions fully. The point is, if you have a relative with both Alzheimer's and victim mentality, they lack the ability to change their thinking, so compassion is all we can offer. For the rest of us... mind your mind.

Victim mentality creeps into our thoughts and words in the form of excuses; all the reasons we have for not being happy, or not doing what we want with our lives. For every solution, there's a problem. To be empowered means we have to completely accept our situation, and then act where we can to change it.

It is a mixture of old teachings and new... Buddhism tells us to just accept what is, and New Agers tell us to actively create our reality. Empowerment requires both. Fully accepting where you are, without resistance, removes fear and the expense of energy on struggle. Then taking action, no matter how small, to change your situation activates your free will. Free will is like the power switch of the Universe.

Something to watch (listen) for is using victim language as

currency. Caroline Myss has written about people using illness as social currency. Really listen to what people are using as currency... always telling you how broke they are, or how hard life is, or any number of stories. I'm not talking about sharing parts of their life in a general conversation; I'm talking about those people who have A TOPIC, that you know will come up, and will be discussed at length. Like your Great Aunt who always has to itemize her illnesses, medications, and procedures, and is offended if you don't ask about her health.

This isn't a judgment, just awareness. Just be aware of the words people use to identify themselves, and their unwillingness to change. Even though they ask for help solving their problems, no solution is ever good enough. They don't want a solution, they want sympathy for a problem. A solution would require change, and generally, suffering is preferable to change. Suffering is a known factor, while change requires faith and a willingness to explore the Mystery of possibility.

Now, turn all that inward. Listen to your own self-talk. Do you make excuses for your unhappiness? Replace "I would do this, BUT..." with "I would do this, *BUT I am choosing to be a victim of circumstance.*" How does that change the excuse? It is no longer a justification, but a choice. When you are ready, you can make a different choice.

Enablers are yet another aspect of this situation. Victim mentality, like so much, is just an addiction. And like any addiction, it requires a supplier. So while you may think you are just being compassionate company, you may actually be feeding an addiction. On one hand it's a win-win, because Great Aunt Lulu gets to feel loved for her aches and pains, while the niece gets to feel useful by listening and making appropriate sympathetic noises, but no one is growing. At an ego level, being an enabler can be rewarding... but at what cost? Again, just be aware of the energy exchange, and how it perpetuates the issue.

As with so much, just the awareness of the dynamic will

allow it to shift. You might easily change a few thought patterns, and then really get stuck on one. That's okay. Just sit with it, and accept where you are. Letting go of the struggle allows things to move. As you work this out inside yourself, you will begin to become more aware of the language others speak. Who are you surrounded by? What kind of stories do they replay? Remember, we become who we spend time with. Look at your 5 closest friends to see who you are becoming. Most of all, mind your mind.

"Above all, be the heroine of your life, not the victim."
~ *Nora Ephron*

"Watch your thoughts throughout the day and you will see a map of your future staring back at you."
~ *Daniel Levin*

DRINKING DICHOTOMY

I was raised in a house without alcohol. It wasn't shunned in any way, it simply wasn't there. I did my fair share of drinking in my 20s, as is customary, but the social drinking continued for my friends. I never liked the taste, and after my decade of various levels of occasional intoxication, I slowed way down. Now I just don't drink. As a result, I don't enjoy being around it. Drunk people are only fun if you're one of them.

Alcohol and social drinking have been a pondering of mine for years. Why do people do it, really? And why am I considered judgmental for asking that question? Why is it a given that people almost always require alcohol to classify something as "a good time"? And why doesn't it work that way for me? Aside from the fact my liver is pretty vocal in its objections, I just don't feel like it is a good time when I drink. I always feel drained the next day, and it's not just physical.

My pondering and observation have led me here: People drink socially because they want to let their guard down, to feel more connected to others, which generally happens after the first drink. But no one stops at one drink. The dichotomy begins to appear in the second drink, when the ability to connect with others, and even with your own body, start to diminish. Words begin to slur, and verbal connection is compromised. Eyes blur, focus is lost, and heart connection is compromised. Thinking gets fuzzy, and mental connection is compromised. After the first drink, the whole reason for drinking has dissolved into unchecked emotion, babbling communication, and liver damage. Dichotomy.

My Grandpa was always known for telling amazing stories of his adventures. He was definitely a larger-than-life character. He kept our guests entertained until the wee hours of the night, without a drop of alcohol. This was the example set for me. The grown-ups were laughing and smiling, and fully present at all times. Blurry eyes just meant it was time for bed.

My disdain for drinking isn't because of a negative judgment; I just miss the connection of being fully present with people!

When I encourage others to stop drinking, it's my own inner child saying, *"Don't leave! I was having so much fun with you! Please stay present with me. It's okay to be real without being numb. I want to stay connected."* But I also believe in free will, and I know most people's parents set the example of social drinking. I don't feel judgmental in any way, just sad that they feel alcohol will enhance the situation, when it only blocks true connection. So, I leave early, and usually read or meditate, so I can at least connect with me.

Again, awareness is the key to everything. If you drink at all, ask yourself why. Is it just habit? Is it fear of connection or depth? Is it rooted in addiction? Is it tied to your beliefs about being an adult (good or bad)? Is it just what people do? Is any of that a good enough reason to keep doing it? Also, stay sober a few times and observe what happens to connection as the drinks flow. Then, at the next gathering, join in the drinking and really be aware of your own energy and reactions. Two things I can tell you without a doubt, no matter what the reasons for imbibing, alcohol lowers your vibration and damages your body. Period. It simply isn't good for your body, so figure out why it's part of your lifestyle.

No rush, when it's time to quit, you'll quit. Just shine some awareness on the whole thing. Know that it's perfectly okay to be deep and connected without alcohol. In fact, it's the only way you can be.

I'm waiting to be fully present with you...

"We need people in our lives with whom we can be as open as possible. To have real conversations with people may seem like such a simple, obvious suggestion, but it involves courage and risk."
~ Thomas Moore

CHOICE OR REACTION

Remember the old placement tests at the beginning of the school year to determine what class you would be in? We're doing that right now. We do this all the time.

In truth, we are constantly changing levels, based on our vibration, and situations are regularly being presented to make us consciously choose a response. As these situations arise, the emotional triggers are automatic, but the key is what you do with them. The usual reaction? Unconscious knee-jerk? Awareness of another option? It is basically an awareness test. It works like this... The trigger happens, we feel it deeply, and then we have a slight pause before we react to decide if we want to make a different choice. The key is in the pause... that's the opening of awareness.

Don't get down on yourself for the trigger or the flood of emotion - those are pretty automatic. The important part is awareness and action. When you get triggered, feel it deeply, and really be conscious of how it feels, and where it's stored in your body. Then just stop for a minute. Feel it and let it go. Then, consciously choose your next move. For me, this has been a lot of short meditations and reframing mentally. My go-to emotion is anger, and silly little things sometimes set me off, just to bring awareness to deeper issues I'm ready to release. Please remember the trigger and the emotion aren't "bad" - you didn't miss the ascension boat. This is about choosing and owning the actions, words, and thoughts that follow.

No one is judging you, or tripping you up. This is just an awareness boost. Awareness and responsibility allow us more access to our free will, which allows us access to higher time-lines. This is just helping us to take advantage of the higher vibrations available to us. Your Soul is pushing you to grow, that's all.

Some people won't notice the pause, the choice point, between trigger and reaction. Some will only see it in hindsight.

And some will seize the moment, to redirect fate. None of these options is wrong. People are where they are. It's important we accept that everyone is on his or her own path. If you want to kick it up a notch and push your own growth, be aware of the pause. Choose, don't simply react.

"There's going to be stress in life, but it's your choice whether to let it affect you or not."
~ *Valerie Bertinelli*

"The self is not something ready-made, but something in continuous formation through choice of action."
~ *John Dewey*

33

CHOICE

CHAPTER 3 - CHOICE

~ Being That Weirdo ~

I kind of lost it on my cousin, Tara. At that point, she wasn't able to hear her intuition, and I was still acclimating to being in service to mine. We had a bit of a clash...

Tara had been working on creating a protective energy bubble around herself, with limited success. She then went on vacation, where a complete stranger walked up to her on the beach, and said, "Try a rainbow bubble," and then just walked away. After she told me this story she said, "But I've always been a weirdo magnet."

That's when I lost it.

"Well, let me tell you what it's like to be that weirdo. He was walking along enjoying the beach, not a care in the world, and his guides say *tell that woman to try a rainbow bubble*, and the argument starts.

What's a rainbow bubble? What does that even mean?

Just tell her to try a rainbow bubble.

She's a total stranger! What will she think?

Just tell her to try a rainbow bubble.

No! I am having a perfectly fine day, and I'm not going to embarrass myself! Again!

Just tell her to try a rainbow bubble.

You guys aren't going to shut up about this until I do it,

are you?

Just tell her to try a rainbow bubble.

Well, shit. *Approaches stranger and says* "Try a rainbow bubble."

Walks rapidly away, trying desperately to cling to a shred of dignity, and disappears to avoid the stares of concern and judgement. So much for his nice day.

"So, his enjoyable time on the beach ended abruptly because he had to deliver a message. If people like you would just listen to your own intuition, people like me wouldn't have to do it for you!"

Even I was surprised at how much this triggered me. When I first decided to simply follow my intuition, wherever it may lead, my ego wasn't comfortable with it at all. I had no problem following my intuition in my own life, but it was a struggle being open enough to share the information I got. Being "that weirdo" was a stretch for me. Not anymore. Obviously.

Listen to your own intuition - save a weirdo.

*"Listen to your intuition.
It will tell you everything you need to know."
~ Anthony J. D'Angelo*

SELF-MASTERY & PSYCHIC ABILITIES

It is critical to note that self-mastery and psychic abilities are **NOT** the same, nor does one indicate the other. Many of us believe that someone with psychic or energetic gifts is somehow more spiritually advanced, and that simply isn't true. This isn't about "we are all equal", this is about avoiding the pain of "following" someone you feel is advanced, only to find out their ego is running the show. Be aware of the ego, both theirs and yours, and don't be blinded by super natural abilities. Some people are just more psychic than others; it is **NOT** a sign of accomplishment or advancement.

I have worked with many gifted healers, readers, teachers, and channelers who are absolutely amazing when they are tuned-in to that high vibrational place, but in their daily lives there are no signs of a higher vibration. It can almost seem like a different personality altogether. There's nothing wrong with living in this kind of polarity, but it can bring disillusionment and heartbreak to those around them. Just be aware of who you are dealing with (the human ego, or the Higher Self), and set boundaries accordingly. Just because someone is psychically gifted, doesn't automatically mean they are a nice person.

Self-mastery is a goal we can all work toward, but it is always work. By that, I don't mean it is difficult, just that it requires conscious effort. It's about awareness, and processing your own psychological baggage, instead of just expecting others to carry it for you. Self-mastery is conscious digestion on the emotional and mental plane. It takes vigilance at first, but once you have formed the habit, it's just a mode of operation. Anyone can learn this, and while it makes life smoother for you and those around you, it may not lead to psychic gifts. The less noise your mind makes, the easier it is to hear your intuition and develop your abilities, but that in itself isn't the goal.

The ego is basically the buffer zone between the body and

Spirit, and consists of the stories we build our life around. It's really the only piece that needs awareness and attention, because the body is always striving for life and health, and Spirit is always striving to be in body. It is only our stories, our egos, which block the natural flow, and require our conscious attention. There can be an increase in psychic ability as self-mastery increases, but again, natural psychic ability doesn't indicate any level of ego awareness. Be careful.

The ego isn't a bad thing, it just requires care and training. Otherwise, it simply repeats old patterns, and perpetuates old beliefs. Your ego (or personality) isn't fixed, and you most definitely have the power to change it. It comes down to awareness and action. Using the body as an example - once you become aware your diet of fast food is harmful to your health, you can then take the action of changing your diet. It's the same with the ego. It's that simple, on paper, but in both cases, addiction (to foods, or chemical-producing emotions) can be an issue. Humans are just prone to addiction, but awareness can enable other choices, including seeking help with your process.

Be especially careful if a person presents their abilities as a sign of spiritual prowess. This indicates spiritual bypassing, or a spiritual ego, which just means their ego-identity is all tied up in their abilities. They feel spiritually superior, and they tend to charge a lot of money for their time. I'm not against charging money, unless they try to tell you they have the one, true, secret way to spiritual success. I charge for my classes, for my time and materials, but the Higher Teachings are available to anyone, with enough meditation. They just fall into your head, eventually. Is the short cut worth paying for? Usually. Is it necessary? Nope.

All of us filter everything through our ego, and I'm not saying that's bad. It is totally normal. My warning is about those who are unaware of their ego's influence, and not getting too close to them. Remember, people can be an asset without being an authority. Take the information that serves you, with gratitude, but don't place anyone on a pedestal. In my own experience, I am a pretty clear channel, yet my ego personality is a bit dark and cynical. Integrating those two is always a journey, but without a doubt, it's possible. Awareness. Do I still have a dark side? You bet. Do I still bring through some helpful and healing stuff? Absolutely. We are all both. Just be aware.

The big things to watch for, in yourself and others, are judgment, dogma, and lack of discernment. Judgment says you aren't doing something the right way. Dogma says their way is the only right way. Lack of discernment says anything goes, because everything is good. In my experience, we all have slightly different paths to follow, but judgment is just ego-based fear, and not everything is good for us. No one is keeping score, but there are things that will evolve you, and things that won't. Free will is all about choosing things that evolve you, and keep you on your unique path, thus making life smoother.

Keep your eyes open, your awareness on, and your personal discernment engaged. Take what serves you, and leave behind anything that offends your soul.

"The highest truth cannot be put into words. Therefore the greatest teacher has nothing to say. He simply gives himself in service, and never worries."

~ Lao Tzu

FREE WILL

More and more I am receiving these messages as suggestions of vague ideas, rather than the normal channeling. I have come to understand this is meant to engage my free will, and to encourage me to actually embody these vibrations, rather than just be a conduit. This is happening to each of us, in our own way.

Along with this, timelines and dimensions are merging, and becoming more available. It can be disorienting, but coupled with free will, it's an incredibly powerful time. Everything is changing, and if things in your world aren't, then it is only because your stories are holding them in place. Right now on this planet, we have access to unprecedented powers of creation. Many, who previously never had the ability to see the future, or experience different dimensions, are now doing so regularly.

We are being given access to this new level of experience and information to develop our free will. Every action, every spoken word, and for some, every thought help to mold the future. Yes, this has always been the case, but now we can know how something will play out before we choose it. We are now in a place to choose which timeline we want to embark on. This is huge! Let this sink in, and really be aware of it in your daily life. Notice how, right before you speak or act, you can tell how things will work out. This moment of clarity allows you to make a choice, thus engaging your free will.

It's a whole new level of personal responsibility, which is the basis of personal power. The vibration of the collective consciousness has risen high enough to allow for this shift in responsibility. Collective consciousness does **NOT** mean the masses of humanity, many of which are still asleep. It just means the bar has been raised for those who are awake, allowing us new areas to explore and new ways to expand.

It is also worth mentioning that you can't exist on two

timelines simultaneously. You must release the old, if you want to embrace the new. You must give up old stories for a new reality to form. Attachment is always a limit, whether it's attachment to the good or the bad, it creates a restriction. Obviously, attachment to the "bad" (pain, fear, mistrust) is what we all need to release first, but to be truly limitless, you must also release attachment to the "good".

The entire world is in the midst of all these changes. Plan on seeing many cultural norms changing. The big ones will be power and control (religion, government, and money), which will completely change the way we relate to each other. This is already apparent in personal relationships, and it will grow. As always, you are loved and supported in higher realms at all times. Please remember to call on your Guides, Guardians, Angels, or whomever you work with to assist you daily. At this point they are only a breath away, barely concealed by the veil. You are so loved. Thank you for your service.

"God is not willing to do everything, and thus take away our free will and that share of glory which belongs to us."
~ Niccolo Machiavelli

DOING & BEING

I know I've talked about this before, but it is so strong it's worth repeating. Like the Gemini twins, or the Masculine and Feminine energies, or the two pillars depicted on the tarot, we live in a world of polarity. In order to integrate these two sides, we need to master them both. This is a bit tricky, because we naturally favor one side. Are you always doing, and have trouble sitting still? Or are you happiest being, and find it difficult to take action? Knowing where you are is the first step in finding balance.

Some people have such a firm belief in fate, they take no personal responsibility for their lives. "It's what's meant to be" is their motto. The other side is totally about personal power, and making life happen. They are both right... and both wrong. *Free will and fate aren't mutually exclusive - they are in a constant dance of creation.* Even when fate is leading, free will must follow the steps or be dragged. There is never a time when you get to "sit this one out". Even consciously waiting for a sign is an act of free will.

If there is one thing I've learned in working with timelines it's that there's always more than one option. Yes, there is comfort in believing what's meant to be will always happen, but we have a great deal of choice in how it happens. Conversely, we can't stop fate, but we can join the dance, instead of incessantly whining that things aren't going as we planned. We need to strive for the balance of doing and being, free will and fate, action and receptivity. This is the Divine Union of your own Masculine and Feminine energies.

Make time and space to rest and receive intuition (feminine), then act on those messages (masculine). An imbalance in your feminine energy will probably show up as an inability to sit still and receive (meditation, a hot bath), where an imbalance in the masculine energy will be inaction, or acting only toward personal desires while ignoring intuition. Yes, both sides can be imbalanced, and it's normal to wobble back and forth while you are learning to balance them. Just keep conscious of the two, and you will get better with practice. It's a journey, not a destination.

Oddly, or perhaps obviously, in my experience it is usually men who lack doing, and women who lack being. Usually. It isn't gender specific in any way, but in a broad scope men are struggling with masculine energy (action), while women are struggling with feminine energy (receptivity). That is most likely a result of social norms being so far askew from the natural state. Just an interesting observation. Interesting to me, at any rate.

Something else that keeps coming through is responsibility. Not just taking responsibility for your own energy, but also taking responsibility for who you surround yourself with. You are solely responsible for the energy you put out into the world, and also for keeping your circle clear. If a friend isn't growing at the same rate, the most loving thing you can do, for both of you, is create some distance between you. Let people be where they are, and be willing to keep going without them. If you try to keep them close, you will feel disappointed, and they will feel judged. Take responsibility for leaving. Step into your life.

Explore these concepts. Start a dialog with your body and your Higher Self, asking, "What do I need to be doing right now?" Then listen for the answer, and act on it. Practice being, then doing. Enjoy the dance of fate and free will.

"I do not believe in a fate that falls on men however they act; but I do believe in a fate that falls on them unless they act."
~ Buddha

THE EMPATH & THE NARCISSIST

There are so many articles out there right now about the toxic relationship between an empath and a narcissist, obviously written by those who have been hurt, and feel manipulated and betrayed. I have a different take on the situation. Saw that one coming didn't you?

First, let's change the labels of the groups. No more good vs. bad stuff. Instead of empath we will say awake (soul driven), instead of narcissist let's say asleep (ego driven). Language matters. We can reduce the polarity, as well as provide a much more accurate assessment. Not only that, but I personally know people who are empathically gifted (they can physically feel other people's emotions), but are very much asleep.

Second, know that all of us operate on a sliding scale between the two, and we change position regularly. We can be very awake, then suffer a loss (like a death or an illness), and go back to sleep to avoid the pain. People self-medicate all the time with alcohol, social excess, and promiscuous sex, to avoid living consciously. Being awake can be tough. We all check out from time to time.

Third, and probably most importantly, we need to understand that most manipulative behavior is subconscious. People (generally) don't consciously manipulate; that takes much more energy and planning than most are even capable of. The ego, however, has full access to the power of the subconscious, and will do anything to avoid harm. All of us are manipulated by our own egos, to some extent. It still isn't right by any means, but thinking someone is consciously manipulating you is giving them way too much credit (and power).

Communicating with those still asleep is almost impossible, at least about anything important to the relationship. Ego defenses go up, and rational thought goes out the window. This is where we get all the passive-aggressive behaviors, and the emotional manipulation. Ever try to voice a concern about your feelings, only to have your partner turn it around, and point out how hurt they are? This is the kind of subconscious behavior that runs the muggle world. You can't break through their ego shield, but many of us keep trying for way too long. Another issue is projection... mostly on the part of the awakened person. See, we think projection is limited to negative stuff, but it isn't. As we awaken, we get more sparkly, and we tend to see our own Light reflected in others. We see Light that hasn't been embodied yet. The fact is everyone has an amazing soul, but not everyone lives from his or her soul. When you begin to live from your own soul, you see the highest potential in others. I don't mean, "He would be so successful if he just had some confidence." I mean, "Wow! He embodies the Divine Masculine!" In reality, he could embody Divinity, if his ego wasn't running the show. It is entirely up to us to distinguish soul potential from embodied reality.

I think the hardest part for the awakened one in these relationships is taking full responsibility for getting sucked in, having to leave, and not repeating the pattern. In other words, it requires us to awaken even further, become more aware, and reclaim our personal power. It's tough to admit there were signs you ignored. It's not fun to know you allowed this damage to happen. Forgive yourself. Forgive yourself for being human. We all do crazy things for love, even forget who we are. You always get lessons in the process. You will heal.

Instead of a list of things to avoid, I want to offer a few things to pay attention to. As we become more aware, we can make choices that support our evolution.

Do actions and words match the sparkly soul? We all have off days, and no one is perfect. But, is there constant negativity going on, in word or deed?

Are words followed by action? Do they do, or just dream out loud? We all need a little daydream in our lives, but plans require action to materialize.

Are they consistent? Again, we all have off days, so

don't expect perfection. But, intermittent reward is a major ego trick. If some behavior is really important to you, and the other person agrees to it, it should be a permanent change. If it only changes briefly after a fight, that's a big sign.

Is communication open? Are you comfortable raising concerns? If your communications are filled with tears, blame, and guilt, then there isn't much actual communication going on.

Do you both own your baggage? We all have baggage. But, insisting one person carries the load for both of you is completely unreasonable.

Are you both dedicated to becoming better people? If you are both dedicated to your own evolution, then you can help each other grow, instead of tearing each other down.

There are those who see the signs, but think they are strong enough to wait for the person they love to wake up. It just doesn't work that way. People don't wake up by following your example. People wake up by shock. Keeping someone safe in a relationship is just giving him or her a warm blanket to keep sleeping under. I'm so sorry – this one is really hard for me, too – you can't awaken someone before they are ready. Ever. And forcing yourself to stay at a lower vibration will cause suffering and illness. It just does. The only way out is out.

The awakened soul must reclaim their power by forgiving themselves, being clear with their boundaries, and letting go of those who are still sleeping. You will heal. You will love again. But first, you must come to terms with the situation. Leave them to their slumber, and move on. Reclaim your power.

"Every man must decide whether he will walk in the light of creative altruism or in the darkness of destructive selfishness."
~ Martin Luther King, Jr.

LOVE & BOUNDARIES

Forget about 50 words for snow, we need 50 words for love, and even then it would fall short. It's difficult to fit an experiential thing into the limits of language, but until we get better at telepathy, it's all we have. Let's try to keep it as simple as we can, and just look at 3 broad categories: divine love (unconditional), human love (conditional), and karmic love (attachment). In my experience, these are the big ones.

The most unfortunate part of this subject is that most people mistake attachment for love. This is just karma playing out. Karma is simply an unconscious vibration or story, but it runs our lives until we become consciously aware of our choices. It doesn't matter what the story is - knight in shining armor, or drunken abuser - only that it is running the show until awareness takes over. If both parties are running on autopilot, karma just plays out, then repeats. If one of the parties is awake while the other is not, then it's a painful, if not abusive, situation. This is where we get all the writings about 'the empath and the narcissist' we see today. It is entirely up to the awake party to leave the situation. The sleeping person is just playing their karmic role.

Karma and attachment aren't about penance for past downfalls, this life or last. It's simply a call to awaken your free will. Karma will keep repeating until you become aware of the cycle, and choose to stop it. Awareness and action are all that are required here. Keeping a journal, and rereading it regularly, will be helpful in identifying patterns. Deciding to act differently, to actually invoke free will, takes dedication. Most people don't want to put forth the effort to change, because they aren't sufficiently miserable yet. Status quo seems better than growth. That's just the way people are by nature. Once you become aware, you will have to leave those who still choose to sleep.

Human love is less common, and requires both parties to

take an active role in knowing themselves, so they can each come to the relationship as a whole being. We can't know anyone else until we know ourselves, or we fall into the karmic pit of projection and blame. This level of love is what we consider mature and lifelong, whether we are talking about siblings, friends, or spouses. As humans, we are each individual, and require strong boundaries (conditions) to function at our best. Some say that only unconditional love is true love. That may be, but relationships require conditions.

Consider how many conditions we have in every successful relationship. I expect my friends to treat me with respect, which includes being honest but tactful, letting me know if they have to cancel plans with me, and keeping promises. I expect various things from different types of relationships, and this is a good thing. Boundaries are absolutely required for healthy relationships.

Acceptance, or non-judgment, is a totally different thing. I can accept that someone has a heroin addiction, but still refuse to be his or her mate. *Loving someone where they are is one skill. Limiting their influence in your life is another.* You aren't judgmental, or in any way less loving, by carefully choosing who to be emotionally close to. That's actually my measuring stick. If I can't be around a person without constantly judging them, then I need to let them go, and redefine my boundaries with them. Judging does neither one of us any good, but creating enough space between us to allow for acceptance will heal us both. Boundaries are vital, and only you can adjust yours.

Divine love is the truly unconditional stuff. This one is hard to describe, because most have no reference to it at all. When you are suddenly awe-struck by a beautiful flower, this is unconditional love. The flower has made no specific effort, and you have no expectation beyond the present sense of bliss. This is harder to do with other humans. Usually one or both of you have some kind of expectation. But still, there can be fleeting moments of nothing beyond the present bliss.

Although we are heading towards the experience of Divine Love, the bulk of our work is shifting our experience from karmic love to human love. Awareness breaks the karmic cycle, free will lets us choose to love at the human level, and all human relationships require boundaries. Strengthen your boundaries to strengthen your experience of love.

"We accept the love we think we deserve."
~ Stephen Chbosky

"Daring to set boundaries is about
having the courage to love ourselves,
even when we risk disappointing others."
~ Brene Brown

CO-CREATION

CHAPTER 4 – CO-CREATION

~ Mateo, Mi Amor ~

Every time I think my life couldn't possible get any weirder, something like this happens...

A fellow energy healer had reached a plateau with one of her clients, and asked me to step in. No problem. Usually a little psych-k does the trick, and puts people back on track. I arranged the session with the client, and did my work (all remotely). Payment was to be delivered in person by her husband, Matthew.

When Matthew showed up two conversations ensued: ours, and the one in my head. The verbal one between us was simple, and lasted only seconds. "Hi, I'm Matthew. Here's the payment for the energy work. I hope to work with you also, maybe in the spring, when I'm ready. Thanks." All I said was "hi" "thank you" and "looking forward to it." In my head, it was much stranger... *Who is this guy? Why do I feel like I need to know him? Should I ask him in? No, that's probably weird. I hope he really does show up in the spring.* Then he was gone, and I shut the door, a bit bewildered. That was December 2016.

The problem with psych-k is that it aligns you with your true self, with no regard to the illusions you have built your life upon. After doing a core belief balance with his wife, her whole life shifted. A Twin Flame appeared for her, she divorced Matthew, she accelerated her healing journey, and started a new life. When Matthew contacted me in May 2017, he was single and starting his own journey.

When he was ready for his own core belief balance, he asked if we could do a trade of some kind instead of cash. That works. I dislike turning people away, and I had a whole list of honey-dos I needed help with. I did my work (again remotely), and he came over a few days later to change light bulbs, re-move cobwebs, and help me scrub grout. I literally said to myself *I'll never see this guy again, so I'm not even going to bother to put on a bra.* And I didn't. I spent the day in my pa-jamas, cleaning and having relaxed conversation. I really enjoyed his energy, but had no plans to ever see him again.

Then it got weird. The next day he asked if he could come over with dinner and a movie. Um... sure, I guess. And this kept happening. For weeks. One day I woke up with my heart chakra all open. When it didn't subside I had to run through a self-diagnostic... *Heart chakra open, giddy, optimistic... am I in love? Am I in love with Matthew? Well, that can't be appropri-ate! Not sure why, but still...*

Fun side note: I got a reading in the fall of 2016, telling me that a romantic interest was on his way into my life. My silent response: *Well, he'll have to show up at my door, be-cause I'm not going to put myself out there.* My Guides silent response to my objection: *Hold my beer, and watch this!* Seri-ously. He actually showed up at my door. My life must be fun to watch from the outside.

I know I'm all in love, and therefore automatically biased, but Matthew really does have an amazingly clear and bright energy field. He exudes a purity and innocence that come across as a bright white light. I was never that pure, even on the day I popped out into the world. Whatever planet he's from is really beautiful.

We had already planned to attend a yoga retreat in Guatemala together in July, so I would have a travel buddy. The week before our trip, we had "the talk" about where this thing was going. We decided to give it a go as a romance. That timing worked out well. We were officially a couple for a whole week before our first travel adventure. Guatemala isn't really accessible with a walker, and even though the retreat center assured us it was, there were more stairs than I could count, and Matthew ended up carrying me on his back all week.

While we were there, we got a Mayan astrology reading. The shaman doing the reading kept telling me, "He brings peace. He's your prince." The prince of peace? I've been getting a piggyback ride from Jesus all week??? So then I kept hearing 'Personal Jesus' by Depeche Mode in my head. The shaman also kept saying that seeing us together gave him hope. It's always a good sign when you give a shaman hope.

On the plane ride home I asked Matthew, "Are we going to pretend this isn't happening, or are you just going to move in?" He replied, "I think I'll just move in." So here we are, a year of adventure later, and still loving every minute of it. We are both learning so much, as we walk this path together. This feels like my first truly "free will" relationship - no karma, no codependence, no contracts, just conscious commitment. It's weird without all that other stuff. Like support and freedom at the same time. I didn't even know this was an option. Life is surprising like that.

"Surprise is God's way of saying 'hello.'"
~ Joan Chittister

SELF-LOVE & SELF-WORTH

I have been asked many times, "How does one learn to love themselves?" A very interesting topic, indeed. I have found that self-love is a function of self-worth, and self-worth comes from validation. Those who have issues with self-worth tend to seek outside validation, while those who have an inherent sense of self-worth find validation within. So yes, once again the answers you seek are within you, but how do we get there?

First of all, leave all delusions behind. Lots of people claim to have a positive body image, when in actuality they want to justify not caring for the body, by eating a poor diet and not exercising regularly. Be careful what you label as positive. Right now we have a lot more justification than love running around. Love promotes health on all levels - physical, emotional, mental, and spiritual. Indulgence and addiction simply aren't loving.

Hedonism is defined as the doctrine that pleasure or happiness is the sole or chief good in life. This leads people to find external validation through stimulation of the senses, which results in low self-worth. Eating healthy food may not give the instant sugar high of cheesecake, but it is an act of love toward your body. Pleasure and happiness are experienced through the body, but only when it's healthy. If your liver isn't happy, your taste buds are serving your addictions. Be honest with yourself.

External validation may also include friends, career, status, and anything else we like to call our circumstances. Not that these things don't matter at all, just that they don't define you. I had a friend tell me, "I have really great friends, so that must mean I'm a good person." While I firmly believe in looking outside yourself for a reality check, I would never suggest you do it to figure out who you are. Outside circumstances change all the time. People lose jobs and get divorced. Don't get attached to any external situation. Build a really good relationship with yourself, your soul. The only person guaranteed to be with you until you take your last breath, is you.

So, then we come down to how to make the switch to internal validation. This has always been helpful for me, and I am hoping it sparks something for you...

Treat your body and ego like a small child or animal. I consider my body like a kitten. You wouldn't feed a kitten cheesecake and rum, because kittens need proper food and water. If a kitten makes a mistake, you wouldn't yell at it, you would keep teaching it with correction and positive reinforcement. I know this may sound a bit strange at first, but really notice how you treat yourself. Then, compare it to how you would treat a kitten. Most of what people do to themselves they would never do to another. When you put yourself in the role of caregiver to your body and ego, you can fulfill your own need for external validation. You become external to the ego when you identify with the Higher Mind, or observer consciousness.

This will assist you in redefining "you" as your soul, not your ego. And there's the key. The soul is our Divine spark, perfect and eternal, inherently worthy. Your body is temporary. Your ego is just thoughts and chemicals. But, your soul is made of pure Divine Love. If that is what you consider "you", then self-love is a given. Your work then, is identifying as your soul. You are a spiritual being having a human experience, not the other way around. Realizing this makes all the difference.

"People think, 'Oh, I'm loving myself by sitting on this sofa for four hours.' Love yourself enough to get up!"
~ *Alison Sweeney*

SELF-CARE

I'm pretty sure we all know the basics, even if we don't do them. Taking care of yourself includes a healthy diet, regular exercise, and plenty of sleep. We understand the physical part. Most of us even understand the mental and emotional parts: be aware of what you read and watch for entertainment, avoid drama and negativity, even carefully choose what music you listen to regularly. All this has been said; you are what you consume, on all levels. I want to take the discussion a little deeper.

Balance. Balance between your own masculine and feminine energies. By being the observer and director of your life, you can protect the feminine sacred space (boundaries), while guiding the active force of the masculine (action). *Boundaries and action.* That's the energetic blueprint of self-care. Think of a child. The womb is the safe space for new life to develop. Even after the child enters the world, it must be nurtured and guided before it is ready to embark on its own adventure. Many of us go about life in the opposite manner, running off in all directions, without the protected space and guidance required for lasting success.

Your feminine energy is the part of you that creates a space, first in your mind then in your schedule. It needs to hold that space to encourage and guide the masculine energy of action. For example, you want to start a yoga practice. First, the idea forms in your mind, until it is so strong you do some research, and can see yourself doing yoga. You are mentally creating a space for something to grow. Then, you make room in your schedule to go to class twice a week. You are creating a space in your life to guide and encourage this new endeavor. Actually showing up and doing it is a result of your masculine energy of action. Boundaries and action.

Why break it down this way? Well, all too often we aren't able to create lasting change, and without sufficient understanding of the process, we simply fall into shame and guilt, only adding to our frustration. By taking a step back into the role of observer, and seeing the process of change as a dance of inner energies, we allow for a new awareness.

Because our egos are so good at illusion and distraction, it's also worth mentioning what self-care isn't... *Checking-out isn't self-care.* A night on the town getting drunk, vegging out in front of the TV, or treating yourself to the extra slice of cake, isn't self-care, it's checking out. Anything that results in a hangover or bloating, isn't care. We all do this to some degree, so don't judge yourself. Just don't mistake it for caring for yourself.

Pampering yourself may be included in self-care, but be sure it isn't the whole package. Trips to the spa, or a weekend retreat make great additions, but they don't make up for daily wear-and-tear. Good food, plenty of rest, meditation, and some sort of physical activity are a daily ritual of self-care. If you are always running yourself ragged, but you think it's ok because you get a massage every week, you are using that massage as recovery. The goal is to make a life you don't need to recover from.

And don't forget joy. Laughter, connecting with friends, gratitude journals, and anything that lifts your heart. This may seem like a lot when you look at it as a to-do list, but it's really an outline for a lifestyle. Self-care is right up there with shadow (ego) work in creating an amazing life. You'll be spending every tiny moment with yourself, so it's totally worth it. Balance boundaries and action. Take care of you.

"Take care of yourself — you never know when the world will need you."
~ Rabbi Hillel

BEING FULLY HUMAN

I know a teacher who says she teaches humans how to be gods. My niche is a bit smaller. I teach gods how to be human.

For many years, I had a great fear of being human, mostly because the people around me who were telling me I needed to be more human were totally ego-bound - lost in addiction, drama, and attachment. After much observation, I have decided that type of behavior isn't "human" at all, because to be fully human we have to balance two things - the physical body and the Higher Mind.

The body is full of chemical reactions and genetic memory. The Higher Mind is the observer consciousness (not to be confused with the monkey mind of the ego). Combining the two results in a human... a real, full, true human. Most people at this point (2018) are still functioning at the more primal (or animal) physical and ego level. I generally refer to them as "muggles" (non-magic folk, from Harry Potter). They just aren't awake yet, and their Higher Mind (Higher Self, intuition) is still too quiet to be noticed.

The Mystery School side of this is fascinating. The body is your feminine energy, and the Higher Mind is your masculine energy. This has absolutely nothing to do with gender or gender roles, and everyone has these two energies within them. Please keep this in mind as we continue, and reread this paragraph anytime you feel triggered in a gender wound way.

In many religious teachings, the body is shunned, as are women. From Eve eating the apple, to women being property, to witch burnings, all things female have been framed as weak and immoral. From a Mystery School perspective, we can see that the body, without Higher Mind guidance, is basically an animal. It's hairy, and smelly, and has hormones to assure continued reproduction of the species. From an animalistic point of view, there is nothing wrong with any of that. Animals aren't immoral, they're amoral. They are driven by instincts and chemicals, without much thought of consequence.

This is why so many New Age teachings say the feminine energy is wild and unpredictable. It's Nature. It's our primal, physical side. The problem is, the body is also prone to addiction, and it houses the ego. Thus the issues with the Hedonistic ideals of placing pleasure above all else, as the primary goal of life.

There's not much to say about the Higher Mind, except that it longs for a physical form to inhabit. Being fully human allows that to happen.

Now, reframe these biblical concepts with the above in mind:

In the beginning, God created the Earth (a physical platform to descend into)

Adam was lonely, so Eve was created from his rib, as a companion (the masculine energy (Higher Mind as Adam) entered the physical body (physicality as Eve), to become one)

Men should be the head of the household, while women should obey his commands (your Higher Mind should lead your physical body, to keep you from addiction)

Go through every misogynistic religious teaching you've ever come across, and retell it in the form of combining your own two polarities. It's truly a shame religious writings are now taken so literally. The symbolism is where the gold is.

So where are you in this balancing act? Is your body (and ego) leading the way to drama and addiction? Is your Higher Mind still yearning for a physical home? Your body is a Temple... cherish it, repair it, clean it. It is host to your Higher Mind. When body and Higher Mind meet as partners, it is true Divine Union. And this, my friends, is what it means to be fully human.

"The greatest tragedy in mankind's entire history may be the hijacking of morality by religion."
~ Arthur C. Clarke

INTEGRATION OF THE TRINITY

It's time for us to master integration. This applies to every level, every part of our lives. Integrity is when your thoughts, words, and deeds are all in line. Now it's time to bring them all together. Any part of you that is out of alignment will show itself for correction.

This process comes to me visually as an integration of the trinity, because in my experience there are always three parts at play: one higher, one lower, and one unifying the two. The Divine Masculine and the Divine Feminine unite to make the Divine Child, which is the same as saying Spirit and Body combine to make a Human. We need both the dark and the light to create our world, but no longer in extreme polarity.

Polarity is the play of opposites - light & dark, spirituality & hedonism, male & female... the list is long in a world based on polarity. Duality is separation - man from God, me from you, you from your higher self... it's an illusion of the ego, designed to allow this journey into polarity. Polarity and duality are represented as the fall from Grace. At the present, we are moving back into a place of unity. Polarity and duality are being replaced with integration and unity.

This integration and unity will happen both within and without. As you integrate the layers within, your outer world will shift. Let it. People and situations will naturally change to reflect the inner work. This has always been the case, but it will now be pronounced. If anything feels wrong or out of place, work to integrate within. We like to think changing the circumstance (relationship, job, location) will fix the issue, but when we integrate within, all those outer things change by themselves, in amazing ways.

The body is a major focal point, because this is a physical ascension process. This means the changes are anchored through your very cells. The best thing you can do for yourself at this point is to foster a loving relationship with your body. The body has its own trinity of voices (at least mine does), and you need to listen and discern. For example, the lower body is full of cravings and addictions *("I want a bacon cheeseburger!")*, the higher body is the light body *("I want water and sunlight!")*, and the integration point is the healthy physical body *("I just want a hard boiled egg and a salad. Sunlight sounds good, too.")*

Get to know your body, and to recognize which voice you are answering to. Here's a hint: The body wants to be healthy. If it is constantly screaming for unhealthy foods or habits, then examine addiction, and get the support you need. Here's another hint: The healthy body voice doesn't generally scream. It's the quiet, small voice, asking for reasonable support. Once you find that healthy, middle voice, it's easy to keep an open dialog. Giving your body proper support is crucial. It is doing some heavy lifting with ascension, and using your free will to support it makes all the difference. I ask my body several times a day, "What do you need right now?" and it generally tells me.

Not everyone will arrive here at the same time. So, have compassion with all, including yourself. It's a journey. There is no room here for helping or saving, only for leading by example. We used to experience being human as a bipolar ricochet between highs and lows, benevolence and addiction, but now the middle ground will be our primary experience. Time to integrate our higher minds and lower bodies to become the Humans we were meant to be.

*"We are three dimensional beings:
body, mind, spirit."
~ Laurence Fishburne*

DEEP HEALING

I was struggling with how to write this, for the healer or the one being healed, but we are always both. So, it should be examined from both sides. *Healing happens when we are fully seen, fully heard, and fully accepted (without judgment).* A person can only meet you as deeply as they have met themselves, and you can only receive healing as deeply as you've met yourself. So, the potential for healing comes from within, no matter which side of the equation you're standing on.

A healer is able to fully accept the current condition without judgment, while simultaneously holding the vision of perfect health. That's not as easy as it sounds, because we live in a culture of "fixers". If something needs fixed, it is obviously broken. To a healer, nothing is ever really broken. You aren't less than what you should be. You just took a different path for a while, and maybe forgot your own perfection. Receiving healing requires acknowledging your own perfection, independent of present circumstances.

To be able to witness a journey (yours or someone else's) without judgment takes much dedication and practice. We are so conditioned to "fix", that we have lost the art of witnessing. Ills, on many levels, are immediately improved by just being fully present to witness the process. Encouragement and support are sometimes best when silent. It takes practice, but witnessing your own journey, without judgment, is the best thing you can do for yourself. It allows all kinds of things to come and go, without attachment. It returns us to the flow of life itself.

"Fixing" is a dynamic, requiring both parties to be attached in a dance of codependency. The one being fixed is placing all their personal power outside themselves, which leads to blame and a victim mentality. The fixer either needs to feel needed or enjoys holding the power of the role. Both fixer and victim are ego-based roles. It is a flawed dynamic, that can only provide limited, and short term, results.

"Fixing" also implies arrogance, resulting in a major power imbalance. This situation says, "They need me! What would happen to them if I wasn't here?" Healing can only happen from within, and personal power is a must. By thinking someone "needs" you, you are affirming their victim mentality, and feeding the codependent role of powerful fixer and pitiful sick person. It's a lose-lose situation. Yes, we all "need" other people in our lives as support, community, and remembrance, but as soon as they become your savior, the balance is lost, for both parties.

"Healing" is about remembering. A true healer holds a frequency, and a vision, of your perfection. No matter their chosen modality, results will hold strong, if you are able to receive their frequency. A healer is simply someone who reminds you of your own wholeness, at least on an energetic level. Healers want you to heal, they don't want to build a clientele. This doesn't mean results are instant, or that you need to limit your visits. It just means that their goal is wellness, not the steady income illness provides.

They say Love heals, and this is true. The unconditional kind is a vibration, not an attachment. The more unconditional love you can pump through your system, the easier it is to heal and be healed. The opposite of this is fear, which usually manifests as judgment. Love unites us at a higher level, while judgment brings separation and isolation. Internally, do you judge yourself for not healing? This, in itself, may be the biggest block.

Healing takes integrity and personal responsibility on both sides. Both parties need to be wary of codependency and attachment, and be willing to stop the treatments at any time, either temporarily or permanently. Healing is a return to your natural flow, so be willing to flow. Use your intuition, and act from sovereignty. Sometimes, a healer feels obligated to work with anyone who knocks on his or her door, but this isn't help ful if you aren't a good match. It's okay to send people on to someone more suited to their needs. It is actually better for both of you.

One of the most powerful healing practices I have found is Ho'oponopono, the Hawaiian healing method. You can just do this for yourself, for any issue – physical or psychological. Just close your eyes, center yourself with some deep breaths, and visualize the issue (your liver, your boss, your former lover, whatever), and say the following four statements slowly, pausing between to let it sink in...

I'm sorry
Please forgive me
Thank you
I love you
Then repeat each statement, one at a time, and give the other party time to respond...
You: I'm sorry... Your liver: I'm sorry...
You: Please forgive me... Your liver: Please forgive me...
You: Thank you... Your liver: Thank you
You: I love you... Your liver: I love you

Any body part, any person, any issue, any archetype, even any sense of Deity. This simple technique can clear the way for healing to happen.

Forgiveness and gratitude pave the way for Love, and Love heals. Then, you are in a position to attract people and modalities to assist with your process. Healing always begins within... and it's a beautiful thing to witness.

"Love is the absence of judgment."
~ Dalai Lama XIV

65

EXPRESSION

CHAPTER 5 — EXPRESSION

~ LOVE SPELLS ~

Several things happened at once in the fall of 2015. I did a complicated ritual, spanning a moon cycle, Halloween, and my birthday, with the intention of bringing in my perfect life. My due date came for a baby I had in a dream. And, unbeknownst to me, a love spell was taking place about three hundred miles away. Possibility danced. Fates coalesced.

My ritual, though long and drawn out, only served to focus my intent and trajectory toward my perfect life. I really didn't have any expectations of what that would look like, and being open to the unseen possibilities is where magic happens.

The baby dream happened months earlier, but with a specific due date. The father was Steve (my second twin flame, whom I had never met in person), and my deceased Mom was there comforting me. You see, I have a habit of figuring out astrology and numerology in my dreams, and I wasn't happy with either. I kept crying about how I couldn't raise a daughter born only two days before my own birthday, because she would be too much like me. My Mom smirked, with maternal irony, but then comforted me.

When the due date came around, I was a little stressed about how my ritual was going to shift things. True to the Great Mystery, Steve and I had one of the best conversations we had ever had, and he unequivocally declared me a guide to him, nothing else. Every twin encounter comes with a hope of some fairytale ending, so I was a little heartbroken at first. Still, it brought clarity and freedom to our relationship. Great baby to have.

Five days after the "baby", and three days after the conclusion of my ritual, I happened upon the most interesting comment on a friend's social media page. She posted something about Isis being an ancient Goddess not a terrorist group, and someone replied, "I agree! The terrorists should be called IS-holes!" I totally need to know this guy. I did some digging, and found we had several mutual friends, because the year I left my childhood town he moved there, just in time for high school. Seems safe. I sent a friend request.

Shanon and I started messaging online right away, and it really escalated quickly. He was talking about wanting me to live closer by the end of our first day of conversation. At this point, I feel it's important to note that I am not easily swayed by men, or by words. I had spent years working in a male-dominant industry, and I'm pretty sure I don't have a romantic bone in my body. The reason our conversation was unsettling, was that I could feel him. It was warm and safe and beautiful... and not like me at all. It was like we were connected... like... NO! Not another twin flame! Not cool, Universe, not cool!

Over the next week, our communication became telepathic. At one point, I was basking in the warmth of his heart, when suddenly I felt a wave of anger. I immediately texted, "You ok? What happened?" He replied, "I just burned myself getting something out of the oven. I'm ok." It was that clear and that intense. I was still postponing talking on the phone, because I didn't really want to deal with another twin. Years ago, a friend told me of her situation of finding a third twin flame, refusing to step into the relationship, and suddenly losing that person in a freak accident. She had always regretted her decision. I knew I'd have to talk to Shanon at some point, because the alternative was too gruesome to bear.

It took me a week to finally agree to a phone call, and I was quite angry by the end of it. I can tell way too much about people when they talk, and even more about a twin. I knew manipulation was his primary coping mechanism, and he mostly pointed it toward himself. I'm not triggered by manipulation, and there are worse things. So, I decided no one is perfect, and pressed on with the relationship. Turns out, manipulating oneself is just denial at its finest. There's no working with that one. But I digress...

When I went to meet Shanon in person, nothing added up. His words said this, but his actions said that. Then I met his friend, Bobbi. She was amazing, and a powerful witch. Something started tugging at my awareness, but it would take another month and another visit to put all the pieces together. Shanon had known Bobbi for twenty years, and he had spent the last eight years in a really abusive marriage, which he was just leaving. Like any good friend, she wanted to help. When witches help, it's best to expect the unexpected.

Bobbi didn't really know the daily workings of Shanon's life, so when he said he wanted a soul match, she made that happen. Problem was, he wasn't living from his soul, and my soul just didn't work with his ego. The funny thing about magic is you never really do a spell for someone else, without it also affecting you. Bobbi also had a twin flame show up in her life. Cosmic humor, there!

I don't believe I was ever intended to meet Shanon in this lifetime. Free will matters, and love spells work. Still, my heart healed, and I don't regret it at all. He's safe now, and back on his journey. And I found Bobbi, whom I simply couldn't imagine living without.

We accomplished quite a lot in our three-month romance. Shanon finally broke free of his abusive relationship. There was lots of space clearing and cord cutting, and even an entity removal. I got to learn so many things, and be near a twin. Mostly I got to see how a love spell works... from the inside.

"That old black magic has me in its spell,
That old black magic that you weave so well;
Icy fingers up and down my spine, The same old
witchcraft when your eyes meet mine."
~ Johnny Mercer

"In all things, it is the beginnings
and endings that are interesting."
~ Yoshida Kenko

TALK & LISTEN

As the veils between worlds thin, we are being asked to actively seek a relationship with our unseen support team. This includes Guides, Guardians, Angels, Ancestors, your Higher Self, and many others. This is also a great time to commune with Elemental energies, Gaia, and inter-dimensional beings of all kinds. But you have to start the conversation, and then listen to the reply.

Humans have an individual crown veil (ego), and also an inter-dimensional veil (space-time) separating us from everything else. Humans also have free will. While the inter-dimensional veil is thinning, we each need to actively seek communication and support from our unseen Team. Talk to them out loud, like they are right in front of you. If you can't sense a response right away, just be observant of what happens around you, and what thoughts come floating into your head later that day.

Listening can be a bit tricky, and gets easier with practice. But the talking part is just free will, just deciding to try it. Why out loud? Because it is time we recognize them as actual beings, not some imaginary friends. They are real, they are here with you, and they want to show you the love & support you have around you at all times. Use your free will to use your voice. Then listen to what they have to say.

Don't confuse this with what we normally consider prayer. No cowering and groveling, they are your peers. Speak to them directly and respectfully, just as you would a beloved friend. And no wish lists - they aren't Santa Claus, either. Praying may sound like, "Please help me get a new job" and true communication would be, "I am really struggling in my job. Please let me feel your support, and show me what I need to see here." Big difference. Then actually listen to the response, whether it is immediate, or in repeated clues. At that point, you again have free will to either follow or disregard their guidance.

Connect. It's like they are banging on the door of your consciousness, just waiting to be invited in. The human drama is much less dramatic when viewed from above. They aren't in the heat of it, so can support and guide with greater clarity than we have. Free will is a thing. Talk and listen.

•••

Unrelated personal note... please vote. Not for any of the usual reasons, but for metaphysical reasons. It is an act of free will and expression. I don't care who you vote for, who wins, or even if it's all rigged, it is still a symbolic act of personal power. Whether you usually vote or not, consider it in this light, and use it to find power leaks in your reality.

•••

"The winds of grace are always blowing, but you have to raise the sail."
~ Sri Ramakrishna

"We should always pray for help, but we should always listen for inspiration and impression to proceed in ways different from those we may have thought of. "
~ John H. Groberg

SPEAKING YOUR TRUTH

This is another one of those concepts that has been adulterated by many in spiritual circles. What it actually refers to is living in integrity. Fully and consciously expressing your gifts, without repression. It has come to mean, however, vocalizing an opinion, or ego-dumping; neither of which are very conscious, or have anything to do with truth.

Society has devolved into communication through opinion, and the loudest ones win. It's a schoolyard of unconscious ruckus, serving no other purpose than ego gratification. I got a wonderful piece of advice from a senior contract negotiator once: "If it feels good, don't say it." I have to admit, that phrase has popped into my head on numerous occasions, and it is always fitting. Ego gratification always feels good. This is the first way to tell the difference between ego and truth. If you "just need to get it off your chest", then it is ego. Always.

This isn't to say that if you are feeling oppressed in some way you shouldn't take a stance. Better boundaries and personal shadow work are probably screaming for your attention, but those are both inner struggles. Don't make them someone else's problem through blame. Blame is simply saying, "My power is getting too heavy for me. Hold my baggage, would you?" Blame is always a relinquishment of personal power, whether it's blaming an individual, a circumstance, a figurehead, or a deity. Accepting your power, in order to operate from integrity, requires a commitment to self-work. Know thyself, and then make the appropriate adjustments. *After some of the personal shadows are cleared, and better boundaries are in place, you may be surprised how little you actually have to say to the people in your life.*

One last thought on ego-dumping... you can't un-ring a bell. Once you have spewed words in anger, there may be apologies and forgiveness, but you can never take those words back. Children are extremely susceptible to harsh words, but they affect even the most stoic among us. It is irresponsible, and just plain mean, to expect others to deal with your shadows for you. Some say this is what relationships are for. If you believe this, ask yourself why. Conditioning? Old patterns? Hurt people, hurt people. Healed people, heal people. *Heal yourself, before you speak. It's that simple.*

Speaking your truth is really about fully being who you are, at a soul level. This may involve art or activism, or both. The only person stopping you, is you. You may be silencing yourself by choosing to be close to people who strongly disapprove of who you really are. If you are gay, but choose to hang out with conservative religious folks, then you are building your own cage. It's ok to let go and move on. *This is the real work of speaking your truth - embodying it.* You need to take responsibility for creating a space to flourish. Only you know your truth, and only you can express it.

Boundaries are a big deal here. Instead of thinking of it as keeping "bad" influences out, think of it as making a strong circle to hold the "good" close to you. Surround yourself with supportive people. Prioritize your schedule to include what keeps you truly fulfilled. Take small steps each day, even just mentally, toward the future you. Use your energy to focus and discover and create your truth. Look at situations that make you feel repressed or stagnant, and take personal responsibility to change them. Change is a good thing in personal evolution.

With all the shadow work and letting go involved, speaking your truth is usually a long and difficult process. People who encourage you to "just speak your truth" don't really understand what they're saying. It may take years of shedding old beliefs before you even know what your truth is. That's ok. Then it may take several more years for you to accept that you need to find a tribe that supports you. That's ok, too. All this change and letting go really isn't that hard, once you start to accept yourself. As your free will begins to align with Divine Will, your frequency begins to change, and life changes with it. Don't focus on the outside, just bring yourself into integrity.

No one else has your gifts. No one else expresses the same way you do. Your voice is vital. Speaking your truth is living as your higher calling. It's walking the walk, when the ego just wants to talk the talk. You are needed, you are supported, you are loved. Let your voice be heard.

"Be Impeccable With Your Word. Speak with integrity. Say only what you mean. Avoid using the word to speak against yourself or to gossip about others. Use the power of your word in the direction of truth and love."
~ Don Miguel Ruiz

TRUST, BETRAYAL, AND FORGIVENESS

This discussion is limited to healthy, adult relationships. This is not about abuse in its many forms, which is never to be tolerated. If you are being abused in any way, the most loving thing you can do, for both of you, is to leave. If you are recovering from abuse, take what you can from these words, but please seek further assistance in healing the trauma.

We have all experienced a betrayal of our trust in a relationship. Betrayal hurts, so very deeply, and always makes us wonder if we will ever trust again. I would suggest that if we allow ourselves to learn from the experience, we actually become more trusting, if less naive. You only have three basic responsibilities in a relationship: communication, boundaries, and managing your own energy. Well ok, both communication and boundaries are really just taking responsibility for your own energy.

Communication means clearly stating your needs, expectations, and disappointments. No one can read your mind, but most can read your energy. If you are obviously angry, but verbally saying you're fine, you are sending mixed signals. Be honest. It's perfectly ok to say, "I'm angry, but I don't want to talk about it yet," but it's never ok to lie. Lying is unfair to both of you. If your normal reaction is to lie about your feelings, it's time to ask yourself why. What are you afraid of? What are you attached to?

Boundaries are essential to every healthy relationship. Strong boundaries are the only way to avoid codependence, and come naturally with self-knowledge and self-respect. First, you must know yourself to know your boundaries, then you must be willing to take action to defend them, which may involve leaving the relationship. First, identify the boundary that has been crossed, communicate the issue, and be fully aware of future transgressions.

Everyone makes mistakes, and should be allowed to correct their behavior. The problems start when the behavior isn't changed and keeps recurring. So many of us then justify the issue with "they are trying to change". Be honest with yourself about how deeply you feel the transgression, and if it is recurring. Sometimes people are just incompatible, and that's okay. It's okay to let people go.

This brings us to the crux of the issue. What story were you attached to that they couldn't fulfill? And what story are you now attached to that keeps you from letting go? Expectation is the leading cause of disappointment, and only you control your expectations. I'm not saying that other people can't do unjust things. Free will matters, and sometimes other people use theirs inappropriately (like infidelity). Even so, you are always in control of your own stories, and it's those stories that keep the unhealthy attachments in place. Even if you are out of the unhealthy relationship, are you still holding on to the hurt or the anger? *What you are really holding on to is a story, an unfulfilled expectation.*

So the question of trust comes to this... Do you trust yourself not to make the same mistake again? And do you trust yourself to heal? Not repeating the same mistake is a matter of awareness. Know thyself. Be totally honest with yourself. Delusion and denial will only keep you bound to the same karmic loop, but the cycle is broken by awareness. It takes courage to be honest with yourself. Be brave. As far as healing, we are built to heal, on all levels. Only our attachments keep us from healing. Find the story and let it go, and healing happens naturally. You are stronger than you think.

Then we come to forgiveness. This one takes a bit longer, because so much has to happen. First, throughout the whole process, you must feel everything. This alone keeps many from forgiving the past. It's a messy business, this emotional muck, but to be cleared, it must be felt. Next, you must identify the stories you were attached to, and grieve their loss. This will require some brutally honest soul-searching, and more emotional turmoil. Not fun, but totally worth it. Last, you must forgive yourself... for getting into this situation, for not seeing the signs, for not leaving sooner, for thinking you could "make it work", for everything you went through by staying, for ignoring your intuition... for everything. We are all imperfect. You are allowed to make mistakes. Forgive yourself for being human.

Then let it go.

You have learned so much from this experience. Keep the lessons, and release the attachments. If things resurface, just keep processing them as they come - feel it, grieve it, and let it go.

Quite possibly, trust is really about trusting ourselves to respect our own boundaries. Betrayal is an unfulfilled expectation. Forgiveness is the messy work of sorting out the first two. Attachment isn't love, yet it's what we build so many of our relationships on. Love yourself enough to see the difference.

"The weak can never forgive.
Forgiveness is the attribute of the strong."
~ Mahatma Gandhi

"The best way out is always through."
~ Robert Frost

CREATION & CREATIVITY

When we think about creativity, we automatically envision painting, or singing, or dancing, or some other form of art. The word "creation" might smack of religion, or some origin story. In the spiritual community, creativity is generally associated with the sacral (2nd) chakra, along with sex, and some muddy darkness that can't quite be defined. I want to take you on a journey of possibility, to reconsider these ideas. As usual, take what's helpful, and leave the rest.

Unconscious creation is how nature exists. Growing a baby doesn't take conscious thought, it just happens. Plants grow. Animals procreate. Nature happens. What if the second chakra is just about creation of physical life? That creation energy would control the hormones and genetic expression, with the primary goal of keeping the cycle of life going. It is a vital function not to be understated, but it is a subconscious physical process. Karma and childhood conditioning are stored as cellular information, and are therefore also part of the subconscious.

The art we associate with "creativity" is always a conscious expression, because it requires a conscious decision to make it and share it. I'm not saying all art is of a high vibration. I'm saying that it doesn't enter the world without our applied will. People make art from both Light (Higher Mind) and Dark (ego) inspirations, but it requires conscious effort either way. This is a throat (5th) chakra function. The energy of creation may flow through the 2nd, but human creativity flows through the 5th.

Physical creation is essential, both for new life, and for healing. It requires our support only in giving it an environment to flourish. It doesn't require any direction from us on how to complete a process. The body has its own wisdom. In fact, the subconscious system runs best if we don't try to consciously dictate and control its workings. Shadow (ego) work brings subconscious beliefs into the light of consciousness to be reevaluated. That bit is necessary for spiritual evolution, but the body is fully capable of healing itself, given the opportunity.

So, if the physical has its very own system of creation, that then frees the conscious mind to explore creativity. Every word you speak, every step you dance, every piece of music you sing or play, every kind of art, even every interaction, flows through your 5th chakra of expression. Being fully aware of this fact lets your creative energy flow freely out to the world. Creativity isn't limited to art; your very energy changes the world around you.

Think about this a bit... What if we really are creators in training? This doesn't have anything to do with the 2nd chakra (or sex), because nature has that one covered. What if people are looking to creation (2nd chakra) for their connection to creativity (5th chakra)? What if fulfillment is only found in our own expression of creativity? What if the only part of our very life force we are responsible for is our unique expression? Humans are unique to nature because we aren't just animals; we also have access to the Higher Mind. Combining animal nature and Higher Mind results in the ego. The ego takes some management, but our focus needs to be on integrating the Higher Mind, not playing as the animal.

Another thing this brings up for me is how strange people's energy becomes when their lifestyle centers on sex. This would include sex addiction, promiscuity, pornography, and various sex-based lifestyles and belief systems. Is the constant emphasis on the 2nd chakra also empowering the subconscious ego? Is the obsession with the 2nd chakra an attempt to touch the power of creation (nature)? Is it to avoid his or her own power of conscious creativity? I imagine it's different for everyone. Please don't misunderstand, sex is perfectly normal, and an open 2nd chakra is essential to health. Still, all of that can be done within reasonable boundaries, and without special emphasis. Some folks just spend a whole lot of extra time there, and I'm exploring the possible reasons.

It seems to me, the happiest people are those who are creating something. We all need to spend more time creating. I don't mean do it for a living; I mean do it for a life. Be it a painting or a community garden, when people let creative energy flow through them into the world, everyone wins. Divinity flows through us as creativity. Creativity is a 5th chakra thing. Our throat chakra gives us our conscious expression, which is how creators learn how to create.

"I can always be distracted by love,
but eventually I get horny for my creativity."
~ Gilda Radner

"Art, freedom and creativity
will change society faster than politics."
~ Victor Pinchuk

NEW VOCABULARY

Words matter. Just ask any poet, philosopher, or magician. On the magical side, correct pronunciation and order can make all the difference for your spell. On the neurological side, pronunciation of seed sounds is used to stimulate various points in the pallet, similar to acupuncture. Esoteric teachings show us that each syllable, when spoken aloud, rings through creation with a power all its own. On the side of basic communication, word definition must be agreed upon to properly share a message. I want to look at a more subtle aspect of language, one that matters most in your own self-talk. The vibration of a word can hold an entire internal experience. So, it may be time to examine your vocabulary.

For each set of words below, close your eyes, and use them in separate sentences (examples listed in italics below), to see if they feel different to you. Really feel the experience they produce. Some may be totally interchangeable, without any discord, and some may surprise you. There is no right or wrong. I am just sharing my own discoveries, that may well only apply to me. In some arenas we need brand new words (technology is changing rapidly). Even our daily self-talk can be upgraded to a higher level. The main point is simply to be aware of your word choice.

Gratitude and Appreciation - *I am grateful for this gift. — OR - I appreciate this gift.*

Grateful implies undeserving, but appreciation is empowered.

Healing or Remembering - *My body is healing. — OR - My body is remembering.*

Healing means something was broken, but remembering takes us to our original wholeness.

Teaching or Guiding - *I am teaching a class. — OR - I am guiding a class.*

Teaching involves hierarchy, while guiding is more equal.

Blessings and Namaste – *May you be blessed.* — OR – *The Divine in me recognizes the Divine in you.*

Blessings come from an outside source, while Namaste comes from within.

Learning and Growing – *I am constantly learning.* — OR – *I am constantly growing.*

Learning implies there are lessons, while growing is just expansive.

Victim and Survivor – *I am a victim of circumstance.* — OR – *I am a survivor of circumstance.*

Horrible things may have happened, but do you identify with the loss of power, or with regaining your power?

None of these words are bad choices, and different people will resonate with different ones. Some people work well with the idea of gratitude, but when I was told to use appreciation instead, it was like the world was suddenly easier. Changing your word choice can really impact your worldview. Examining your word choice brings a whole new level of awareness. Awareness makes conscious choice possible.

Word definitions have a vibration. Words construct the boxes for our very existence. Choose your words to create your world. We are all just stories, in the end.

"No matter what people tell you, words and ideas can change the world."
~ Robin Williams

CHAPTER 6 — INTENTION

~ Accidental Upgrade ~

So, Bobbi is a witch. I don't mean New Age Wiccan and a salt circle, I mean 13th generation, magic grimoires written in Greek (where her family immigrated from), and serious esoteric knowledge. We met because of one of her spells, but that's another story (in chapter 5).

She lives about six hours away, so visits are few. When we do get a little time together, we talk for hours, and the time flies by. On this visit, we got to spend almost five hours in deep conversation. Sitting on the couch together, having tea, lots of eye contact... be careful of prolonged eye contact with a high vibrational being... just a tip. It was a lovely visit.

A couple days after I got home, I got extremely sick. Like strep throat and a fever kind of sick. At that point, I hadn't been really sick in a very long time, probably a decade, and even longer since I took antibiotics. I knew it was strep throat because I had it so much as a child - twice a year, the whole time I was in school. Well, this sucks.

I was determined to at least try to deal with it on my own, while knowing a doctor was an option. I really wanted to actually clear it from my system, not just suppress it with medication. I meditated on raising my vibration... and it worked! At least for three hours at a time. I would meditate to raise my vibration, the fever would break, my throat would feel fine, and three hours later I would have to do it all again. Every three hours for three days, but I finally cleared my childhood nemesis.

Somewhere on day two it came to me that this wasn't just some random infection. It was a detox. And not just any detox, but a release of old genetics to allow room for new ones. They don't mention that in science class. New genetics? Like a DNA upgrade? Is that even possible? Turns out, it is.

I contacted Bobbi, and basically accused her of giving me the plague. "Did you do this? What did you give me?"

Flashback: A few months earlier, it had come to our attention that some entities were harvesting human emotion. Basically an inter-dimensional, black market emotions ring. Before you write this one off, think of the energy involved in an emotional outburst. It's like serious drugs to some, both human and not. Bobbi was working closely with Archangel Michael on finding a way to protect people, like an inoculation of sorts. She had been given these codes, but wasn't clear on what to do with them yet. Did I mention the eye contact thing? Yeah.

So we worked out that the codes she was given were passed to me, completely by accident, during our lovely chat. After my detox period, my intuition strengthened impressively, and in about a month, the upgrade started spreading. I would be talking to someone (not everyone, just a few), and my head would tingle and my hands would get hot. At that point, I would explain the upgrade process (detox, intuition, passing it on), and ask if they wanted it. Even the ones who thought I was a little nuts agreed, and we would enjoy a couple minutes of eye contact to let the information pass.

They didn't think I was nuts for long - everyone had varying degrees of detox, which was a nice validation. It spreads by voice and eye contact, and it really is a DNA upgrade. If you aren't ready for it don't worry, it won't go to an incompatible person. I tried. But still, eye contact with a mystic is always at your own risk.

"My life needs editing."
~ Mort Sahl

"The greatest healing therapy
is friendship and love."
~ Hubert H. Humphrey

"Our own genomes carry the story of evolution,
written in DNA, the language of molecular
genetics, and the narrative is unmistakable."
~ Kenneth R. Miller

MEMORY

Memory has always fascinated me. Or at least, most people's lack thereof. I'm only talking here about healthy adults, without any kind of disease or disability affecting the process of memory. Never feeling quite at home as a human, how the mind works is a constant source of amazement. How can some people remember nothing, while others have a photographic memory? More importantly, does it even matter? I believe it does, and that memory is tied directly to spiritual awakening.

All the esoteric knowledge points to memory as a vital part of spiritual development. When we are born we "forget" where we came from, and when we awaken we "remember". No one teaches us anything; they just remind us of what we have forgotten. The story of Isis healing her partner, Osiris, by piecing him back together, or "re-membering" him. Memory is a big deal spiritually, but how does that look on a human level?

We all know the ego likes to mess with our memories, blocking things that differ from our beliefs, and embellishing what supports our patterns. We know that memories change over time, so many consider them unreliable. Here's my current theory: If a person is ego-driven, then their memory is only utilized to support the ego. If a person is less ego-bound, then they are free to remember a much wider array of experiences and information.

We all have that friend who only remembers an experience if it is a peak high or low for them personally, but never has any recollection of what anyone else went through. It's a very behaviorist existence - avoid pain, seek pleasure. Yes, we all do this to varying degrees, but I'm talking about people who live that way most of the time. If memory is only used to seek pleasure, avoid pain, and bolster the ego, we are talking about some pretty animalistic behavior, but it may be a whole new angle on the nature vs. nurture debate.

The people I know with the best memories aren't attached to the experience or information. Numbers are just numbers, facts are just facts, and experiences are just experiences. So, they can remember them all, without picking the ones that support their ego. It's not that they don't have negative experiences. It's just that it isn't what holds their story together. These folks have a sense of self outside of the ego story.

That said, we all fall along a continuum between the two. What's even more interesting, is that we are at different points on the line all the time. Told you memory is fascinating!

This explains selective memory. Some people are great with facts and figures, but can't remember interpersonal details. Are they ego-bound, but the ego has an attachment to being smart? Is their ego only triggered in personal interactions? I know some very intelligent people who do some pretty unconscious things. So, the ego is playing a role.

This also explains abusers. I know a few people who had really abusive parents, and when they tried to discuss the issues (years later, as adults), the abuser had no recollection of the situation. Of course, that's adding insult to injury. But, maybe the abusers were so ego-bound that they truly can't remember the situation. My guess is they never will. I think this is why there is rarely an apology for abuse.

Even though I had an amazing childhood, there were several times I consciously chose to be less conscious, just because being awake was so painful. While I have vivid memories starting around 1-year-old, there are places (after choosing to be asleep) where I have very spotty and vague memories. Even though I am more awake now than I've ever been, with the coping skills to sustain it, I can't get those blank spots back.

Then there is the other end of the spectrum – channeling. When people are so far from their ego, even briefly, they don't have much memory of the information that comes through them. When I write or counsel I only remember broad topics, never detail. In my "human" life I have a detailed memory, but when information flows through me, I can't hang onto it. So either end of the spectrum diminishes memory.

For years, I've believed that high I.Q. is just a good memory. The ability to adapt to new information requires a memory of the old. Finding patterns requires remembering a flow of information. As we collectively awaken, will the average I.Q. rise? Does meditation improve memory, not because of relaxation, but because it reminds us who we are? Sure will be interesting to watch.

Think back on your own memories... why did you pick those ones to hang onto? What areas are you currently trying to forget? Find your own patterns. And most of all, remember who you are.

"Memory is the mother of all wisdom."
~ Aeschylus

"Nothing is more responsible for
the good old days than a bad memory."
~ Franklin Pierce Adams

LOYALTY & ACCOUNTABILITY

I used to think loyalty was pretty simple. You stuck by your friends no matter what. But there has been a recurring theme in my life, since childhood, spotlighting the fact that I have no control over someone else's free will. No matter how much I love someone, I can't stop his or her bad choices. (And just to be clear, "bad" to me just means ego-based or selfish, not morally wrong.)

I am definitely a proponent of boundaries. Unconditional Love requires strong boundaries in conditional (human) relationships. I think where I got lost on this one is thinking that once people are on a path, they stay there. This just isn't true. People wander around quite a bit, and some never return to their original course.

Is loyalty about following them down the spiral? Is it about reminding them of who they were or could be? Is it about holding their space in my Tribe until they return? Or is it more fluid than that? What if loyalty is a dynamic force, and not carved in stone? Unconditional Love only flows out, but loyalty requires presence and action, much like respect. Loyalty is a relationship and requires boundaries, like any relationship. Enter accountability.

Accountability requires personal responsibility and awareness. In my experience, once someone chooses an ego-based path, awareness drops off almost immediately. So, personal responsibility doesn't stand a chance. Once they are ego-bound, they become the classic narcissist, totally asleep at the wheel. It doesn't even matter if I point out exactly where the fork in the road was, they can't see it. At that point they only feel judged due to my sudden lack of support. Enter guilt.

I have always felt terrible about those of my Tribe I have lost along the way, even though they were the ones who left me. I have felt betrayed and abandoned, but also guilty, like I should still be there for them. The guilt comes from an old warrior ideal of never leaving a fellow soldier on the battle-field. But they aren't injured... they chose this new path. We aren't even on the same battlefield anymore. This is why I need to reexamine my thoughts on loyalty.

Maybe it is simply disrespectful to expect people to re-main who they once were. Maybe they were never those people at all, only a projection of my own mind. Maybe it's okay to let people come and go, not just in my general life, but also in my Tribe (Inner Circle). Maybe the concept of loyalty has very little use at all, and really only Love matters.

That I can do. I can completely Love someone, and bless them on their path, even if it is in the opposite direction. I don't feel obligated, in any way, to guide them, or stop them, or wait for their return. I just wish them well, and let them go. Hmmm...

To any of my Tribe who are now on another path: I love you, I wish you well, and I thank you for all the time and ad-ventures we had. In deepest gratitude, I release you to your chosen path. And so it is.

"Loyalty to petrified opinion never yet broke a chain or freed a human soul."
~ Mark Twain

JUDGMENT & DISCERNMENT

As you know by now, I love words, and how we use them to build concepts. The definitions I use aren't the "right" ones, but it's good to be really clear about meaning when you use a word, especially in conversation. So let's explore some words, and the concepts they represent...

First, let's talk about observation. If I notice that you are wearing a blue shirt, we can all agree, that's observation. The confusing part of this concept to me is that if I notice other testable and mutually agreed upon facts, it's considered judgmental. For example, I notice someone is obese, or short, or disabled, or even really smart. Why are humans stuck on the idea that equality requires homogeny? Observation does not include an assignment of better or worse, only defining differences.

Next, I may form an opinion based on my observation combined with my conditioning. For me, I consider the original information to be purely sensory input, until my brain starts adding right and wrong / good and bad. Noticing a blue shirt is one thing, deciding it looks either really good or really bad on that person is another. The longer I dwell on a subject, all the while adding mental commentary, lets me know how strongly opinionated I am about it.

Then we come to judgment. I have spent years trying to decipher this one, and I've boiled it down to this: *Judgment is just a verbalized opinion.* Once your opinion leaves the confines of your head, and enters the world around you, it will be noticed by others. If a person always gives compliments (positive judgments), then people feel relaxed in their presence. If they always criticize, then people feel a bit on edge. One thing is for sure, if a person consistently verbally expresses their opinions, they will express them about you, as well, for better or worse.

Ending a sentence with "but that's just my opinion"

doesn't make it any less of a judgment. Try it on... if someone tells you "your hair looks bad" or "your hair looks bad, in my opinion" does it feel any different? People don't really like to own their judgments, so they soften it by saying it's just an opinion. It gives the speaker a little comfort zone of denial, but the words hit just as hard.

This is another one of those head scratching moments for me. Why do some people feel the need to constantly narrate their opinions? Are they seeking validation? Do they think the rest of us are missing something without their opinions? Do they just like the sound of their own voice? I'm sure it's different for each person, but it's a fascinating thing to watch. Like a blind person touching walls to define the space, their verbal chatter seems to define their world. Hmmm... never a dull moment, watching muggles.

Judgment also involves emotional attachment. It feels sticky. It usually includes "should" or "shouldn't", and can be directed at the self or others. It is generally negative and controlling. "I shouldn't have eaten that ice cream, now I have failed at my diet." "They should go to jail for speaking against war, it's unpatriotic." Lots of misguided control. Lots of condemnation. A black and white view of the world, usually based on conditioning. Pretty unpleasant stuff, really.

Many spiritual teachings warn us to watch our words. Words are powerful magic, both spoken and written. Beyond asking yourself if it is *true, necessary, and kind* before you speak, the deeper concern is asking yourself what your motivation is for sharing. *Why* are you speaking? Are you being helpful or controlling? Are you sharing information to keep people informed, or divided? What is really driving your need to speak? Know thyself.

Discernment is the decision you make for yourself, without attachment to anyone else's behavior. Discernment feels very neutral, with no emotional charge. It isn't a decision that needs to be shared or validated, it's just what's right for you.

Birth control is an area of personal discernment. People try to make it political and emotional, but in the end, everyone needs to make the choice they need to make. When we use discernment, we can see many sides to a situation, we weigh the options, and make a choice with a clear head. Then we let it go. Discernment doesn't have strings attached.

And we just have to mention alternative facts. Those are just lies. I completely understand that "facts" change over time with our scientific perception (the world is no longer considered flat, nor does the sun revolve around it), but we collectively agree on certain things so we can communicate. We should always be open to new possibilities, and keep questioning social norms. But, let's not just start making stuff up to see if it catches on. We collectively agree to call the sky blue, so giving an "alternative fact" of it being orange isn't in any way helpful to communication. Just don't do it. Alternative realities and parallel universes are a different matter, but we always qualify them as "alternative", not "fact".

Then there are theories... like this one. There is no right or wrong, just an attempt to explain the world around me. All I can hope is that my rambling sparks your own thought process. I just want to throw out some possibilities for you to ponder. Do we really spend too much time thinking, or just too much time playing with our opinions? I leave it for you to discern.

"It's easy to judge. It's more difficult to understand. Understanding requires compassion, patience, and a willingness to believe that good hearts sometimes choose poor methods. Through judging, we separate. Through understanding, we grow."
~ Doe Zantamata

EPIPHANY

Epiphanies are just falling out of the sky! Be careful...
once you see something, it's really hard to un-see it. Once
you face the truth you have been denying, the world goes a
bit sideways before you hit the joy of liberation. Let this new
level of awareness flow into your reality, and integrate with
time. Awareness is everything.

When I was a teenager, my Grandma used to caution me
about who I was hanging out with, saying one bad apple can
spoil the bunch. I countered with, "Jesus hung out with lepers
and prostitutes, and he turned out okay." And Grandma would
say, "You aren't Jesus!" I was always offended that she didn't
think I was as strong as Jesus, but now I see it as a different mission. Jesus was a bright light in a dim world. His mission was to be a light for others. Without question, this is not
my mission. All of a sudden "you're not Jesus" sounds like a
great reminder.

The incoming energies require each of us to do the work
to embody them ourselves. No more messiahs. We are the
ones we have been waiting for. If you are holding the Light
for another, think about two things: 1) You aren't Jesus, and
2) it's actually hurting both of you. You are limiting your own
potential by waiting for them, and they will never learn to find
their own Light with you providing it for them. They aren't
being lazy on purpose, but people simply don't see the need
to do the work until they have no other choice. Humans learn
through loss. If you really love someone, allow them to find
their own Light.

Another thing coming through really strong is the message
to look at your friends. Not in a judgmental way, just an eval-
uation. I read an article a few years back about how you can
tell who you will be in five years by looking at your five closest friends. Just take a moment to think about that. Really
look at who you choose to spend time with, and ask yourself

if that's who you want to be when you grow up. If you respect and admire your group, then carry on. If not, figure out why you are there, and make adjustments. Most of us have quite a diverse group of friends, but this is just about the five you spend the most time with.

There are many other personal epiphanies coming in for me, but even those have the main themes of "let people do their own work" and "align with who you want to become". Powerful stuff. Enjoy the energy... and learning even more about who you are.

"It is always important to know when something has reached its end. Closing circles, shutting doors, finishing chapters, it doesn't matter what we call it; what matters is to leave in the past those moments in life that are over."
~ Paulo Coelho

"There are lots of people I admire and respect, but I don't necessarily want to be like them. I'm too happy being myself."
~ James D'arcy

THE ETERNAL NOW

We all want to be more present, but what does that really mean? Like most things experiential, it's easier to talk about what it isn't, and go from there. As humans, we spend most of our time time-traveling. We project our thoughts either into the past or the future, when both are basically imaginary. Yet, it is also folly to completely disregard the past and future. The only point in time you are actually living is right now, but to live meaningfully we must have the context of our total existence.

Being present isn't over controlling or under controlling the flow of life. Being present requires a balanced use of free will (masculine energy, 3rd chakra), and trusting some kind of greater order. *The two most common ways to avoid true presence are:* 1) projecting into the past or future due to an excessive need for control, and 2) completely ignoring the past and future due to an aversion to taking control of our lives. Both over-controlling and under-controlling are an attempt to avoid pain, but both cause greater suffering in the long run.

Over-controlling is excessive use of free will. It shows an unhealthy level of attachment to the circumstances, people, or situations of our existence, either past or future. It may stem from the weight of responsibility, or a sense of having to prove oneself, or an overreaction to victim mentality. Over-controllers think it's all down to them, either all the past regrets or all the future progress, and they tend to believe "life is my creation." This is the result of an overactive and fragmented ego. This tendency to over-control needs to be tempered with Trust... Trust that life has a rhythm and a reason, and this force is active in all we do.

Under-controlling is a lack of applied free will. It shows a basic unwillingness to show up for life and take an active roll in co-creating existence. It may stem from a deep feeling of powerlessness or unworthiness, or an imbedded victim mentality. Under-controllers just want to watch life, rather than participate. They avoid choices (like voting), and they numb out at every opportunity (like addictions), and it is all justified by saying "everything happens the way it is supposed to anyway." This is the result of an under-active ego glorifying animal consciousness. This tendency to under-control needs to be tempered with empowerment... (the basic knowing that each choice matters, and life is always responding to your input.)

Life is always a co-creation. Free will matters. Take action. Divine Will matters. Trust the flow of life. Learn from the past, plan for the future, but live right now. Think of driving a car. You don't stare in the rearview mirror or at the GPS, but neither do you ignore them. You glance at them, but spend the majority of your time looking at your immediate area. Same thing. Don't dwell on the past or future, but glance at them to be sure you are incorporating past lessons, and taking actions to keep moving toward your chosen future. (And, of course, never get distracted gawking at someone else's accident.)

Once you are used to it, it is just habit to glance forward and back before making a choice, just like looking before switching lanes. Before each choice, I quickly ask myself, "Have I seen something like this before? Will this action keep me moving toward my goal?" Yes, before every choice. Awareness is everything. Mistakes still happen, and I add them to my learning experiences. I'm sure it isn't a perfect system, but it frees me to live in the present, within the full context of my life.

"Do not dwell in the past, do not dream of the future, concentrate the mind on the present moment."
~ Buddha

CONNECTION

CHAPTER 7 — CONNECTION

~ A Day In The Life ~

DRAGONS

A group of six of us had a little Merkaba / spiritual training reunion of sorts in October 2017. On the drive home someone asked, "What's that energy following us? It feels really big and powerful." The reply from someone else was, "Oh, that's just my dragon. She's traveling with me." Holy crap! Really? We all had felt the energy, but none of us had guessed it was a multi- dimensional, mythical creature.

Of course, this made me investigate the possibilities... that's just what I do. After much meditation, over the course of a few days, a dragon appeared on my roof. She isn't really "mine". One doesn't own a dragon, but you can attract one.

A few days later, the local homeless guy with a chainsaw, who comes around every few months looking for work, talks my neighbor into cutting down his tree, that's mostly positioned over my house. He asked if he could climb on my roof to do that. I agree, close the door, then think of all the reasons that was a bad idea. Instead of chasing him down, I just asked the dragon to keep an eye on things, and protect the house. Within a minute, the chainsaw stopped. My neighbor told me later the guy's chainsaw broke, and he would be back tomorrow. Never heard from the chainsaw guy again.

It's good to live amongst dragons.

NEVER AGAIN!

A lifelong friend of mine was suffering from some pretty severe digestive issues, and finally called me for help. We lived seven hours apart at that point, but distance healing is my thing. I told him to lie down and relax, and I would work with his energy. About half an hour later he called saying, "It worked! I have no idea how, but it totally worked! *Don't ever do that again!!!*"

Spooky action at a distance is just too spooky sometimes.

THE LIFE OF BOOKS

The last book I wrote, *Waking Up Indigo*, really has its own life. I put the words on paper, but I've never considered it "my" book, and always refer to it as "the" book. It always leads me into crazy adventures.

I was preparing for my weekly grocery run, when I distinctly heard *"Go to the store downtown. A guy needs the book."* Then I saw an image of a young man with dark hair and dark eyes. Grumbling the whole time about my dislike of shopping at that location, I headed for downtown, as requested. I've learned it's just easier to follow my intuitive guidance, even if I have to whine while I do it.

After an exhausting shopping experience, with many items on my list missing from the shelves, I finally made it to the checkout. At this point, I just wanted to go home, even though I never saw anyone needing a book. As the checker bagged my groceries, I asked for carryout assistance. She looked totally shocked at the request (even though I was using a walker), so I said never mind. Just then, a voice behind me in line says, "I'll help her out. I'm only buying a drink, and I'd be happy to help." I turned to look at the Good Samaritan, and see dark hair, dark eyes, and a beautiful, bright, indigo light around him.

After he got my groceries loaded in the car, I gave him a book. Like most, he had that 'what-cult-are-you-pushing?' look, but I told him if it wasn't for him just pass it on. Then I thanked him, and drove away, leaving him a bit bewildered. Yeah, welcome to my world. He emailed later and thanked me. I assume that book is still living its life out there somewhere.

SHAPESHIFTING

I had the first book published before it had much proof reading, just because I had to get it out before I lost my nerve. It was properly edited later, but I had one last copy of the sloppy version to give away. I always carry a few in my car, because you never know when you might need to share.

On my usual weekly grocery run, when the cashier called for carryout assistance, the guy who showed up was this huge Viking, with a big red beard, and an indigo light surrounding him. Ah, he'll do. So, he helped me out, and I gave him my last unedited book. He looked confused. I felt relieved. I could now start handing out the better copies.

About a month later, he emailed me saying, "You gave me your book about a month ago, and my life kind of blew up. Can we get together and talk?" Of course we can. When he showed up at my house, he didn't look anything like I remembered, except for the light. He said the same thing about me. Are we seeing in energy? Are we changing our energy to project a certain appearance? Is that really saying the same thing?

He moved out of state a few months later, but we stay in touch. Brandon is one of those bright lights in the world, with some serious Viking energy.

SYNCHRONICITY

A friend sent me a book that one of his other friends had written. I like books, and I give and receive them often. I wasn't really enthused with the title, The Mature Empath, as I really didn't feel like it would be new information to me. In fact, it took me about two weeks to even open it. When I did... wow! It wasn't so much the information, as the voice of the writer. Someone just like me! Yay!

I contacted Tracy to introduce myself, but it would be another month before I pursued the friendship. I'm weird like that. I can see where things are going, but I have to wait for life to catch up. It's teaching me patience and right timing, I'm sure.

Turns out, she works with physical (body) energy, just like I work with the collective. We are two sides of a coin. Ever since, we have been working together, trading techniques, and having an overall great time. It's so nice to be surrounded by people who live in my world! Your vibe really does attract your tribe... in the most synchronistic ways.

CHOP WOOD & CARRY WATER

Remember the old Buddhist account of Enlightenment? Before enlightenment, you chop wood and carry water. After enlightenment, you chop wood and carry water. My life is truly magical, but only the highlights are worth writing about. There are plenty of days that revolve around the basic chores of existence. Public school was basically a personal hell. On top of that, I can think of three full years (at various stages) that were primarily spent crying in the fetal position.

Every life has struggles, and is packed with ordinary bits,

but never overlook the magic. The Universe always brings more of what we focus on.

"*Every day is a surprise. There are confirmations of an interconnectivity and synchronicity which inspire, titillate and confirm the inherent comedy of the universe.*"
~ *Billy Zane*

"*Miracles are natural. When they do not occur, something has gone wrong.*"
~ *A Course in Miracles*

"*An adventure is only an inconvenience rightly considered. An inconvenience is only an adventure wrongly considered.*"
~ *G.K. Chesterton*

IN SERVICE TO LOVE

As I enjoyed a hot bath on a high-energy day, the information came flooding in. I was brought to tears several times
by the sheer magnitude and beauty of everything I was shown.
We are so limited by language, but I will try to describe the
messages.

My personal story is that I received my mission quite
young, and it always weighed heavily on me. Only in the past
decade have I experienced fleeting moments of this mission
feeling like a gift, an honor. In the last couple of years, those
feelings have increased, in both frequency and duration. Now I
can spend hours in total bliss, knowing that this is how we are
all destined to live. Living a life of service isn't a duty or full
of drudgery. It is an expansive act of becoming. It is to fall
completely in love with being. I don't know if this awareness
is a result of the decades of climbing the mountain, or just an
epiphany, or part of the physical upgrade we are all getting.
I don't know if I was even capable of hearing this when I was
younger. I don't know if it will make sense to you. I just know
it's real for me now, and I know it's where we're all heading.

The greatest service any of us can offer is our own becoming, our own self-mastery. If you think of dedicating your life to
serving humanity and you feel martyred, drained, or even useful (need to feel needed), then you are only serving the ego.
True service is beyond these human states. It fills every cell
and pours out into the world. You can never make someone
else evolve, but by becoming who you really are, you change
everyone around you. You are a drop of water in: the ocean of
humanity, the lake of your community, the bathtub of your soul
family, and the glass of water of your twin souls. Your effect
changes all, but is more potent in your smaller groups.

I am never alone in these progressions, and neither are
you. I speak to a pretty specific group in the first wave. As
this wave ascends, others will need to start speaking to the

next wave, and so on. These aren't clear divisions, and there are always those in-between groups. The point is, if you have been feeling the nudge to start sharing, please do so. It's like a human chain, and we pass our knowledge from one hand to the next. Some will write, some will teach, some will use video... just do whatever you're called to do. Start now.

Remember to use the intelligence of the body to help guide you. Whatever decision you face, see how it feels in your body – expansive and open, or contracted and limiting. If your emotional and mental bodies are clear, they will give the same answer. The problem we face with those bodies is that the emotions, and the monkey mind, get caught up in the fear of change. Yes, even good change will require feeling all the human turmoil as it comes up. The body is a great barometer for decision making before action.

Also remember to talk out loud to your Guides. Once you get into the habit of including them in your daily life, they will start being more present. They will eventually start the conversations. Having a strong team of invisible friends makes all the difference.

Above all, be gentle with yourself on all levels, especially your body. These energetic upgrades are very much physical changes. Even releasing old patterns is a cellular function. Some people will hold on so tightly to their old ways, or their set goals, that their bodies simply won't make this upgrade. You can't make them change. Free will is a thing. The best you can do is lead by example, and be who you truly are.

I feel like I'm rambling and jumping all over. I hope this is of some help on your journey. The ego is no longer being supported, but the beauty of true service is Divine. Be open to the bliss of being in service to Love. Namaste.

ACTIVE SURRENDER

There is so much happening, at so many levels, at different stages in different groups. I will try to simplify as best I can, within the limits of language. 2014 was about surrender to the heart, feeling more, the Divine Feminine. 2015 was about taking action, owning your power, the Divine Masculine. 2016 was Balance of these energies, and 2017 was Union of these energies. 2018 brought Illumination of the Shadow, 2019 brings the Gathering of soul families, and 2020 will be our First collective Steps toward our New Earth. Not everyone is at the same place. This is just the timeline of the first major wave of awakening. Some are still totally asleep, while others are already working on building New Earth. Everyone has a different path.

Many are struggling with ego attachments to the past, clearing old beliefs and karma. The collective ego is now thinning, so those with strong ego attachments are in great suffering right now. The energies no longer support the ego, so their suffering will continue to intensify as time goes on, until they are ready to release attachment to their old beliefs.

What is ego attachment? It's just a story you build your life around. An emotion is a chemical in the body that normally passes fairly quickly, unless you build a story around it, and then it becomes anchored. For example, if your Father was mean to you at Christmas when you were young, you may have built a story about your Dad, about men or about Christmas, and those old emotions are triggered whenever you engage in that story. It is time to release those old stories, both good and bad, to embrace the possibility of something new.

These old patterns will keep coming up, stronger and stronger, until you release them. Releasing them isn't that hard now. Just be fully aware of the belief you're up against. Be gentle with yourself. That belief served you in the past, Now that it no longer serves you, you can simply decide you are ready to release attachment to it. It really is that simple. It may take a few times, and the releasing may bring up new stories to be released, but simply allowing the possibility of something new has the power to change everything.

This is active surrender. You need to take the action of clearing out old beliefs, and surrender to the possibilities, so the Divine can do its job. Every time you catch yourself thinking 'this is how it's always been, this is just who I am', or 'I want things to be like they used to be', just stop what you're doing and take a minute to examine and release these old beliefs. The future is very expansive, and trying to fit into a small box you created long ago will become painful and impossible.

Keep doing your daily practice of connecting to Source, as this will soften and speed this process. You are completely loved and supported. Your Guides, Guardians, and Angels are always waiting for you to call on them. Be gentle with yourself, but also dedicated to the action of aligning with your Higher Self. The shift is well underway. Thank you for your service.

"The practice of being on a spiritual path isn't about being the best meditator or the kindest possible person or the most enlightened. The practice is about surrendering to love as often as possible."
~ Gabrielle Bernstein

ABSOLUTE ACCOUNTABILITY

As you enter into the higher realms of spiritual development, you begin to see the effect of your every thought on the world around you. The awareness actually becomes a bit painful, because not only do you clearly understand your own life, but also those around you, those you love. We each absolutely create our own suffering. It's difficult to watch, and impossible to correct, except for ourselves. You will reach a point in your development when change is inevitable, and change usually costs us some (or all) of our relationships.

This is beyond the dramatic break-up, and the feeling of being alone. This is more of an allowing, and a complete dedication to inner growth. At some point you just realize growth is the end game, and all else is distraction. A convincing distraction, I'll give you, but just a distraction. You come to a complete knowing that everything outside you is temporary, and only the light within is eternal. This becomes more than an ancient teaching, or a mental theory, and you feel it deep in your bones. At that point, you do everything you can to make that small glow a blazing fire.

This awareness seeps into every action, every word, and every thought. You are constantly asking yourself, "Is this evolving me?" It sounds obsessive, but it is really an act of being fully present with yourself at all times. To monitor your every thought as an observer requires complete dedication, which for me is a consequence of Love. This is one of those mystical experiences (a Rumi moment) where the desire for Divine Union (union between body and Spirit) outweighs all else. Once you have the slightest taste of it, it becomes a consuming drive. Presence is addictive.

Presence makes every moment eternal, because you live fully in the now. We spend most of our time projecting our consciousness into the past or the future, enjoying only fleeting glimpses of the present. It is meant to be the other way around. We need fleeting glimpses of the past and the future to remain on course, but life only really exists in the present moment. Yes, learn from the past, and plan for the future, but live in the now. Eternity exists here. Awareness brings us to this zero point of creation.

Living in the moment isn't the same as hedonism. In fact, it is quite opposite. Hedonism asks, "What do *I want* right now?" and Spirituality asks, "What will *evolve me* right now?" Just because an action isn't being judged as right or wrong doesn't make all actions equal. Yoga will evolve you faster than alcoholism. It just will. Neither one is wrong, but by saying, "everything is spiritual", one is missing the point of free will. Discernment is vital to spiritual growth. Discernment and free will guide your progress. You steer your ship, it isn't at the whim of the tides.

Looking at it from the outside, it seems like a list of rules, requiring a great deal of discipline... no drinking, practice meditation, eat lightly, exercise, measure your words... But what if those are just observations of habits of those on the Path? What if these "rules" are really just a "fake it until you make it" strategy? What if, when you raise your vibration, your habits simply change to fully support your body and your life? That's my observation. I have seen many people try to be spiritual by following a list of rules, but people whose light is brightest just live those "rules" because it feels right. They are simply fully accountable to themselves for their own wellbeing.

You are accountable, always and only, to yourself. You can't make decisions based on someone else, nor can you just do nothing, expecting enlightenment to fall out of the sky. Every single action, word, and thought affects your very cells. They change your vibration, and similar vibrations always find each other as people, places, and things. You create your world, both consciously and subconsciously. So, it is in your best interest to bring awareness to all aspects of your being. You are accountable to you.

"There is only one corner of the universe you can be certain of improving, and that's your own self."
~ *Aldous Huxley*

"Life is not accountable to us. We are accountable to life."
~ *Denis Waitley*

"Human beings should be held accountable. Leave God alone. He has enough problems."
~ *Elie Wiesel*

ALIGNMENT

Integrity happens when your thoughts, words and deeds are in agreement. When we take this one step further, we get alignment. The catch is you can be aligned with your ego, or your soul. This is the heaven and hell polarity split. Many people are pretty good about their integrity, meaning their thoughts, words, and actions agree. The question becomes: Who are they agreeing with?

The ego is an illusory fraction of ourselves, and illusions are fading fast. Quite rightly, the ego is afraid of its own destruction. Fears are running really high at the moment, as the ego constructs are falling. The ego simply isn't being supported anymore. That game has run its course. Letting it go will be much less painful than hanging on. Really.

How do you identify the ego? It's the one that acts from fear. My ego prefers anger to fear, but it's a derivative. There are really only two basic platforms to operate from: fear or love. Every emotion we have can be traced back to one of those two states. Fear always contracts, and love always expands. When you think of something, feel how your body reacts. Think of a loved one, and feel the relaxing and expanding sensation. Then, think of politics, and feel the physical contraction. Hierarchy is an ego power construct, and will always cause discomfort, on some level.

Ego death is never a fun process, and grieving is appropriate. Sometimes it is a series of small deaths (of beliefs), sometimes it's all at once. You just don't know you're living in a house of cards until they fall. Just know it is part of the journey, and many have gone before you, and lived to tell the tale. That said, it is indeed a necessary process for human evolution. Plus, it really is pretty amazing on the other side of it.

The soul is always love-based and expansive. The goal isn't to ignore the ego, but to integrate it, as you align with your soul. Yes, you need to vote, and be as involved with politics as you are called to be. Just keep checking to be sure you're aligned within. If you can't just do your civic duty and re-center yourself, it may be time to meditate or take a walk. Everyone gets caught up in the world from time to time. That's totally normal. Just don't live there. Always take time to align with your eternal self.

Why? Because your Higher Self is descending into your body. If you are full to the top with ego, there is going to be a mess when that ego gets displaced. If you are consciously (and constantly) making room, your Higher Self can fit into your life more easily. I wouldn't say it's "easy" for any of us, but it will be decidedly more difficult for the ego-bound. It's happening either way. Evolution happens to us all. Just know you can make it easier on yourself by aligning on a soul level.

Let your thoughts change. Let your beliefs soften. For goodness sake, turn off the TV news. Look within. Spend more time with wonder than judgment. Be in the world, not of it. Still function here, but always return your gaze inward. The outer illusion is crumbling, while the inner reality is blooming.

Align with the future. Align with your own soul.

"Turn your face to the sun and the shadows fall behind you."
~ *Unknown*

BREATH OF GOD

I can only do my best to interpret the visuals and sensa-
tions coming in, and I know words will fall short. This would
be a great time for the telepathy to kick in. I am hoping the
words are enough to spark your own connection, and bring you
the greater understanding that's intended.

Whenever we shine more light, more dark gets illuminated.
It's like going into the crawl space under your house with just
a flashlight, but then you plug in a floodlight. The flashlight
shows you some of the creepy-crawlies, but the floodlight
shows them all. With the flashlight you could pretend there
were only the few spiders shown by the narrow beam, but
there's just no room for denial once the floodlight comes on.
This is what's happening in the world right now. So much light
is coming in, all the darkness is being exposed... and it ain't
pretty.

As the darkness is forced into the light, it will eventually
dissolve. As day breaks, shadows first become apparent, and
then die away as the sunlight spreads. We are witnessing the
dissolution of polarity, as we return to unity consciousness.
This is a painful and tragic thing to witness, and it's perfectly
normal to hurt and grieve. Just know there is so much more
going on than what it feels like on a human level.

On the flip side of watching the horror of the dark come
to light, is the feeling of relief and almost euphoria of the
higher vibration. This is also a perfectly normal thing to feel,
and don't let guilt tell you otherwise. Even though events of
darkness are horrible, on many levels, you sense the incoming
light. For this reason, it's going to be quite a roller coaster
ride for a while... probably a few years. The best thing for you
to do is allow yourself to feel all the ups and downs, without
getting attached to either.

In simple terms, there will be a tragedy, you'll feel really
bad, and the next day you'll feel amazingly good. Just go with

it. Sounds a bit harsh, but we are experiencing polarity followed by unity, and we will feel both. The in-breath and out-breath of God.

At the same time, we can no longer ignore the darkness that comes up. We are being called to action, but not in the old way. Instead of fighting the dark, you are asked to hold the light. Instead of marching in a protest (which isn't a bad thing), maybe plant a garden and donate the food to the poor in your own neighborhood. Step in when you see someone being bullied. Smile at people. Offer compliments and encouragement. Small acts, in your everyday life. This is how we embody the light. "Be the change you wish to see in the world." ~ Gandhi

It's time.

These waves of incoming light will continue, and get even stronger. Remember what's happening. It affects us on a physical level, as well. Be gentle with yourself and others, on all levels. We are in this together. That will become increasingly apparent as the shift continues. You are loved and appreciated. Always.

*"Give light, and the darkness
will disappear of itself."*
~ Desiderius Erasmus

AFTERWORD

Just to tie up a few loose ends from *Waking Up Indigo*...

I finally met Steve (my second Twin Flame) in person, in October 2018. It was amazing, but probably only for me. He was not quite ready to meet me with an open heart, but he still showed up to meet me, so he gets a point for that. I feel like the second half of this story has just begun, so I'll share it when it plays out. And yes, I can tell a Twin by feel. There's just no doubt.

Ataxia is still a thing in my life. As of December 2018, my general health keeps improving, but the ataxia hasn't changed much. Some areas are better, some are worse. I generally remember that what's going on inside is the important part, so I can carry on with my life without being lured into the illusion of physical reality. It's an interesting path. Not much room for wandering off course.

I do plan on future writings. You can also check out my site at www.WalkingInBothWorlds.com for the latest energy updates, and blog posts.

And a special thanks to YOU for joining me on this adventure in time and space. Namaste.

"Set your life on fire.
Seek those who fan your flames."
~ Rumi

Further Exploration

Books:
The Life You Were Born to Live by Dan Millman
The Secret Language of Relationships (or Birthdays, or Destiny)
by Goldschneider & Elffers
Autobiography of a Yogi by Paramahansa Yogananda
Outrageous Openness by Tosha Silver

Movies:
What the Bleep Do We Know? (2005)
Documentaries on Gaia TV

Groups & Teachings:
Gene Keys Golden Path
www.teachings.genekeys.com

AMORC (Ancient Mystical Order of Rosae Crucis)
www.amorc.org or www.rosicrucian.org

The School of Remembering, Drunvalo Melchizedek
www.theschoolofremembering.net

Blogs & Such:
Me www.WalkingInBothWorlds.com
Lee Harris www.leeharrisenergy.com
Sandra Walter www.sandrawalter.com
Patricia Cota-Robles www.ersofpeace.org

Made in the USA
Monee, IL
08 February 2020